50 Short Romance Outlines

~Plots for Contemporary Romance In Duet Pov~

by

Paige Ryland

Popular Author of My Curvy Crush and other Short Romances

Table of Contents

Short Romances By the Author...1

50 Short Romance Outlines | ~Plots for Contemporary Romance In Duet Pov~ | by | Paige Ryland | Popular Author of My Curvy Crush and other Short Romances 4

Contemporary Romance ~ Part 1 9

Contemporary Romance ~ Part 2 40

Billionaire Romance 76

Holiday Romance... 107

Enemies to Lovers & Second Chances 143

Bonus: 10 prompts: Age Gap, Sports Romance & Western 174

50 Names for Romance Heroines 206

50 Names for Romance Heroes...209

Extra Bonus 1 | 25 Ways for Couples to Meet In a Romance 211

Extra Bonus 2 | 25 Settings for Scenes In Short Romances........ 214

~ Thanks for Reading! ~ 217

Short Romances By the Author

My Curvy Crush

PerfectlyCurvy for Him

Perfectly Curvy for My Best Friend's Brother

Perfectly Curvy for My Best Friend

Crushing On Her Curves

My Mountain Man Protector

Briggs: Boss Kink Romance

Copyright 2025

by the author and publisher
All rights reserved
Published by **RSVP Press**
Cover design by **VEB**

50 Short Romance Outlines

~Plots for Contemporary Romance In Duet Pov~

by

Paige Ryland

Popular Author of My Curvy Crush and other Short Romances

Book Blurb:

50 Short Romance Outlines~Plots for Contemporary Romance In Duet Format With Alternating Viewpoints of Heroine/Hero.

Find the plot for your next short romance–even if it's your first romance ever!

If you write short romance or you've always wanted to write a short romance, start with these outlines and use them as is or adapt them to your needs to create stories that grab readers all the way to the HEA.

Whether you're writing a short story or a novella, there are 50 outlines with plots to jumpstart your imagination and get you writing now.

Bring your talent and tell your love story!

Includes:

Contemporary Romance ~ Part 1

Contemporary Romance ~ Part 2

Billionaire Romance

Holiday Romance

Second Chances & Enemies to Lovers

Also Includes: Bonus Content

10 Additional Outlines: Age Gap, Sports Romance & Western

50 Names for Heroines

50 Names for Heroes

Plus–Extra Special Bonus!

INTRODUCTION – Your Ultimate Guide to Short Romance Plot Outlines

Hey there, Fellow Writers!

Whether you're just starting your journey in romance writing or you're a seasoned pro churning out stories faster than anyone can keep up with, let's chat about something that can seriously up your game: plot outlines. You might be wondering, "Why do I need a plot outline?" or "Can't I just wing it?" Well, plot outlines are like a trusty roadmap that keeps you on track while exploring the winding roads of love, heartbreak, and happily-ever-afters.

For those of you who are new to writing romance, think of an outline as your companion in this exciting adventure. It's your guide to understanding the basic structure of a romantic tale. It helps you figure out how to build that sizzling chemistry between your characters, create conflicts that keep readers on the edge of their seats, and craft resolutions that leave everyone smiling. With an outline in your back pocket, you can focus on the fun stuff—like getting to know your characters and bringing their love stories to life.

And for you experienced writers, especially the prolific ones keen on rapid releases, plot outlines can be a lifesaver. You know how fast the romance genre moves—readers are always hungry for the next swoon-worthy story. Having a solid outline lets you work efficiently, jumping between different plots without losing track of what makes each story unique. You can even plan out multiple storylines at once, saving you time and energy when it comes to writing.

But here's the magic: these outlines don't have to be set in stone. You can totally use them as they are (but if you do, be aware that others may as well and that could result in a similar story), or get creative and adapt them to make them your own. Change the names, switch up the settings, add a supporting cast of characters, give your characters new jobs, or even flip the usual tropes around. Epilogues can also be edited or changed. Creating character bios and different backstories can also change the resulting story. With some caution, you can even change scenes (the Meet Cute can be altered without any real altering to the storyline, but be aware,though, that many die-hard romance readers expect scenes like First Kiss and others). Scenes can be added (to add additional depth if desired or needed) or split into two alternating viewpoints (the Meet Cute, the First Kiss or the Intimacy Scene). Make changes to make the outlines *yours*. It's your story, after all! Making these tweaks adds your personal flair, ensuring that your tales of love are fresh and unique. * Note: For same-sex romances, you can usually reassign Hero/Heroine and use the plots with little to no adjustments. There are a couple of same-sex examples included in the outlines.

One major problem with many premade romance outlines is scenes that are not (imo) writable. For example, how do you write a montage? Personally, I don't know. The scenes in this guide are writable for me. If they aren't for you, you can insert a scene that is writable for you as long as it continues the story or fits into the existing outline to continue the plot without being jarring to the reader. All scenes can be changed as long as you can create a replacement scene yourself or drop in another scene from another outline as long as it works with the plot (and yes, you can change the drop in scene to match the details of the story you are telling!)

Stories can start with the inciting incident if you include enough details in the Meeting and include these in her POV or write a scene from each POV so that important details can be included and, thus, relayed to the reader to make the story make sense. If you hold back some background information on one main character (usually the hero, but sometimes the heroine), it'll create a sense of suspense or intrigue in the reader and add interest. Readers are curious to know what is *not* being said, whether it's a secret or just not fully spelled out. Usually the pov character's internal thoughts would skip over some crucial part relating to his/her life and think something 'maybe no one will notice that I have no idea how to do this' or other such thought that hints that something is not quite for right for some reason that will have to be cleared up or explained later.

You can use *knowledge* gaps (a literary device where one character knows something another doesn't) to add interest to your plot and story.

It helps to have a solid start, which an outline can provide. I know because I have used these duet outlines (with changes as noted above) for some of my romances and readers enjoyed them. When I veered off and wrote romances without the benefit of an outline, readers' reviews and ratings indicated they did not enjoy reading the stories as much.

You are what makes the romance story and the romance outline unique.

So, as you dive into writing, remember that outlines are just tools to help you spark your creativity. They're not restrictions; they're ways to help your ideas flow more freely. Allow yourself to play, explore, and, most importantly, have fun with your writing.

You have to add the ingredients to make your romance capture the hearts of readers, but an outline certainly makes it easier.

In a nutshell, whether you're a newbie just dipping your toes into the romance waters or an old hand looking to fine-tune your process, embracing plot outlines can really make a difference. They're your ticket to crafting engaging love stories and capturing the hearts of readers. So grab that notebook, whip up an outline, and let your imagination take flight. You're about to embark on a wonderful journey, and I can't wait to see where your words will lead you! Happy writing!

Best always,
Paige Ryland

Contemporary Romance ~ Part 1

Outline for Behind the Veil

Chapter 1: Intro to Leigh (Heroine)

- Introduce Leigh Bennett, a talented and promising model struggling to find her place in the fashion industry, juggling between glamour and the harsh judgment that comes with it.

- Highlight her vibrant personality, aspirations, and deep passion for charitable work, underscoring the emotional disconnect she feels from the superficiality of her career.

Chapter 2: Intro to Julian (Hero)

- Present Julian Kane, a reclusive billionaire known for his philanthropy but equally famous for shunning the limelight. Explore his complicated history, marked by personal loss and the burden of legacy.

- Reveal his inner struggles with loneliness and the weight of his responsibilities, drawing a contrast between his public persona and private yearning for connection.

Chapter 3: Meet Cute

- Leigh attends the charity gala as Julian's hired guest. The initial meeting is awkward; Julian is reserved and silent as he observes her weaving through the crowd.

- Leigh tries to engage Julian with small talk, but he remains aloof, which only intrigues Leigh more. They share a moment while watching a dance performance, where a spark ignites in the briefest of glances.

Chapter 4: Growing Attraction/Getting to Know Each Other

- Through a series of interactions at the gala, they gradually begin to open up. Leigh relates to the charity's mission, and Julian finds himself drawn in by her genuine passion.

- They steal moments away from the crowd, engaging in meaningful conversation that breaks down Julian's barriers and highlights Leigh's wit and depth, revealing their shared values.

Chapter 5: First Kiss

- During a quiet interlude in the garden outside the gala, Leigh and Julian share their first kiss underneath a starlit sky. It is tender but filled with longing, marking a pivotal turn in their relationship.

- Both are surprised by the intensity of the moment, feeling a connection that carries both hope and uncertainty.

Chapter 6: Her Smell

- As the night continues, Julian thinks about Leigh's intoxicating scent—a mix of fresh flowers and the warmth of her presence. He can't shake the feeling of being captivated by her beauty and spirit.

- His close friend, who notices Julian's preoccupation with Leigh, teases him about being smitten, prompting Julian to voice his worries about the implications of falling for someone from a different world.

Chapter 7: His Taste

- After the gala, Leigh reflects on the kiss while confiding in her sister. She relives the sweetness of Julian's lips and how his kiss felt like a promise—both exciting and terrifying.

- As she shares her feelings, she grapples with the reality of their worlds colliding, questioning if their connection can survive beyond the night they shared.

Chapter 8: Internal Conflict/Resistance to Attraction

- Julian dances between his growing feelings for Leigh and the fear of opening up to someone so different. The pressure of his family expectations weighs heavily as he struggles with the idea of a relationship.

- Leigh reflects on her insecurities, feeling unsure if she can be the woman Julian needs in his high-society world, fearing society's judgment and her own misgivings about their differing lifestyles.

Chapter 9: Steamy Hot Intimate Scene

- After a few blissful yet complicated dates where they explore their dynamic, they find themselves together in Julian's luxurious penthouse.

The simmering tension culminates in a passionate, steamy encounter that deepens their emotional bond.

- This scene emphasizes the powerful release of their pent-up attraction, both physically and emotionally, making them feel a sense of liberation in each other's arms.

Chapter 10: Internal Falling in Love

- As they continue dating secretly, both Julian and Leigh begin to recognize their deepening feelings for one another. Julian sees Leigh as the light that breaks through his self-imposed shadows, while Leigh learns to trust and let someone in.

- Their time together is filled with laughter, shared dreams, and moments of vulnerability, leading them both toward the realization that love transcends their life differences.

Chapter 11: Dark Moment/Pulling Apart

- Just as they think they've navigated their differences, a media outlet uncovers their romance, leading to public scrutiny and judgment. Julian's family pressures him to end the relationship to protect his image, intensifying his internal conflict.

- Leigh, hurt and feeling used, confronts Julian about the very real implications of their romance, leading to an emotional fallout where they separate to reassess their lives.

Chapter 12: Resolution

- In the aftermath of their breakup, both Julian and Leigh go on separate journeys of self-discovery. Leigh dives deeper into her charity work, finding strength in independence, while Julian faces his family's expectations and finally stands up for his own happiness.

- They each realize that their love is worth fighting for. A heartfelt reunion leads to both a powerful apology and the promise to forge their own paths together, breaking away from societal expectations.

Epilogue: HEA (Happily Ever After)

- Several months later, Leigh and Julian are at a new charity event where they co-host together. Their relationship is public, respected, and admired by both the community and their families.

- They stand united, proving that love can triumph over circumstance; they are not just partners in charity but also lifelong companions, ready to navigate the future side by side, filled with hope and happiness.

Outline for Publicity Stunt

Chapter 1: Intro to Heroine (Mia)

- Mia's Perspective: Mia Rivera, a rising pop star known for her infectious hits and vibrant personality, is introduced. Despite her success, she feels the pressure of fame and struggles with maintaining genuine relationships, often doubting if anyone loves her for who she truly is.

Chapter 2: Intro to Hero (Blake)

- Blake's Perspective: Blake Sullivan, the talented quarterback of the Crestfield Lions, is introduced. He is passionate about his team and dedicated to proving himself after a series of setbacks. With a reputation as a flirt, he grapples with his desire to win back the fans' hearts and redeem his image.

Chapter 3: Meet Cute

- Mia's Perspective: Mia and Blake's paths cross unexpectedly at a charity event where they are both present as guests. A mishap—Mia nearly falls off the stage while reaching for a microphone—leads to Blake catching her, igniting instant chemistry and playful banter amidst the crowd.

Chapter 4: Growing Attraction/Getting to Know Each Other

- Blake's Perspective: As they are thrown into their staged relationship, Blake begins to appreciate Mia's talent and her genuine nature. Despite the surface-level interactions, he finds himself intrigued by her ambition and charisma during photo ops, public appearances, and media events.

Chapter 5: First Kiss

- Mia's Perspective: After a successful charity gala, where their chemistry is electrifying, Blake and Mia share a moment alone on a balcony. Amidst laughter and vulnerability, time seems to freeze, leading to a thrilling first kiss that surprises them both and deepens their connection.

Chapter 6: Her Smell

- Blake's Perspective: As their staged romance unfolds, Blake becomes addicted to Mia's unique scent—a blend of citrus and vanilla from her signature perfume. The memory of her smell lingers with him long after their interactions, igniting feelings he can't ignore. One afternoon during practice, he catches himself daydreaming about her, his teammate noticing the dazed expression on his face. You falling for the pop star, Blake? the teammate jokes, which makes him flush with realization—he indeed has it bad.

Chapter 7: His Taste

- Mia's Perspective: After their transformative kiss, Mia finds herself reflecting on the moment alone in her dressing room. She can still feel the warmth of Blake's lips against hers, the taste of his minty breath mixing with the faint hint of whiskey from earlier celebrations. It's a blend that leaves her breathless, and as she confides in her best friend, she admits how the kiss sparked something electric within her—an unexpected crush on Blake that she never saw coming.

Chapter 8: Internal Conflict/Resistance to Attraction

- Blake's Perspective: Despite their undeniable chemistry, Blake wrestles with guilt and fear. He worries about the publicity stunt's authenticity and the repercussions of genuine feelings. Torn between what his heart desires and what the media and fans expect, he pushes back on his attraction to Mia.

Chapter 9: Steamy Hot Intimate Scene

- Mia's Perspective: After a particularly exhausting week of constant media presence, Mia invites Blake to help her relax at her home. They share a passionate moment that leads to an intimate encounter. In that dimly lit living room, surrounded by the soft melodies of her music, their chemistry ignites like never before, leaving them breathless and questioning their feelings.

Chapter 10: Internal Falling in Love

- Blake's Perspective: Following their intimate encounter, Blake can no longer deny his feelings for Mia. He admires her perseverance and heart, recognizing the depth of their connection. He starts dreaming about a future together, realizing he's falling for her in ways he never expected.

Chapter 11: Dark Moment/Pulling Apart

- Mia's Perspective: Just as everything feels perfect, a scandalous article surfaces in the tabloids that misinterpret their relationship, making Mia question Blake's sincerity. She worries he was only using her for publicity, leading to a painful confrontation that drives a wedge between them. Heartbroken, she retreats to her private life, feeling more isolated than ever.

Chapter 12: Resolution

- Blake's Perspective: Determined to prove his love and clarify the truth, Blake tracks Mia down after a show. He passionately declares his feelings for her and explains how she's helped him rediscover his authenticity. Their heartfelt conversation resolves the misunderstandings, reopening their hearts.

Epilogue: Happy Ever After (HEA)

- Mia and Blake's Perspectives: Several months later, both Mia and Blake navigate their careers as a genuine couple. They attend events together, supporting each other's passions—Mia playing a new hit dedicated to Blake, while he shares his latest victory on the field. The media buzzes about their love story, but this time, it's rooted in truth and authenticity. Their relationship is a blend of trust, passion, and understanding, leaving them excited for a future they plan to tackle together.

Outline for Fated Actors

Chapter 1: Intro to Heroine (Jessica Hart)

- Jessica's Perspective: The story opens with Jessica on set for her latest film. We delve into her background as a dedicated, talented actress with a fierce commitment to her craft. She reflects on her past co-stars, showcasing her frustrations and fears about working with Ryan, a notoriously volatile actor. Jessica's desire to prove herself and make a name in Hollywood drives her, even amidst the pressure she faces from the industry.

Chapter 2: Intro to Hero (Ryan Chase)

- Ryan's Perspective: Ryan is introduced as the charming yet reckless actor known for his laid-back attitude and penchant for causing drama on set. He reveals his struggles with the expectations of fame and how he's frequently underestimated by those in the industry. Despite his charisma, he grapples with a profound sense of insecurity about being taken seriously as an actor. His reputation as a troublemaker precedes him, a puzzle he longs to solve.

Chapter 3: Meet Cute

- Jessica's Perspective: Their first encounter happens during a press conference announcement for Fated Hearts. Jessica finds herself poised next to Ryan, who immediately starts joking around, causing a stir. She is annoyed and misinterprets his humor as immature, while Ryan finds her uptight demeanor intriguing. Their clash of personalities sets a combative tone, filling the air with tension that leaves lingering gazes and charged banter.

Chapter 4: Growing Attraction/Getting to Know Each Other

- Ryan's Perspective: As rehearsals begin, Ryan notices Jessica working tirelessly, refusing to let anything distract her. He starts learning more about her dedication and passion for acting, realizing that there's more to her than what he initially judged. They start having conversations that drift away from their film characters, revealing hidden depths, and Ryan finds himself drawn to her intelligence and determination.

Chapter 5: First Kiss

- Jessica's Perspective: Their characters are forced into a heated romantic scene that requires genuine chemistry. The tension builds as they play a couple madly in love. In a moment of vulnerability, during a break, Jessica impulsively kisses Ryan, the electricity between them undeniable. Both are taken aback, realizing that what started as resentment has crystallized into something unexpected and compelling.

Chapter 6: Her Smell

- Ryan's Perspective: After their kiss, Ryan finds himself captivated by Jessica's presence, particularly her unique scent—a mix of jasmine and the crisp fragrance of her skin. Whenever she's near, he feels a swirl of emotions; her scent becomes a comforting reminder of their chemistry. He reflects on how he was wrong about her and how much he yearns to be closer to her, even as they navigate the complications of their budding relationship.

Chapter 7: His Taste

- Jessica's Perspective: After the electrifying kiss, Jessica can't help but replay the moment in her mind. Later, she confides in her best friend, Mia, about how Ryan's lips tasted—like a mixture of mint and a hint of whiskey, which shocked her with its sweetness. Remembering that kiss fills her with warmth and excitement, igniting a whirlwind of confused feelings regarding their professional relationship and this new attraction. Mia encourages her to explore these feelings, hinting at the potential for something more.

Chapter 8: Internal Conflict/Resistance to Attraction

- Ryan's Perspective: Despite the undeniable attraction, Ryan fights against the growing feelings for Jessica, worried their romance would disrupt the film's success. He is also haunted by the fear of being vulnerable, rooted in his past experiences with relationships. He tells himself it's just the adrenaline of filming that's steering him in Jessica's direction, afraid of upsetting his chaotic but familiar lifestyle.

Chapter 9: Steamy Hot Intimate Scene

- Jessica's Perspective: The chemistry explodes into an intense encounter in a private portion of the set late at night, where they let down their guards. Their steamy passion reflects both their worries and desires, intertwining their lives in ways they hadn't anticipated. In this moment, they beat aside their uncertainties and give in to their connections, temporarily forgetting the world around them.

Chapter 10: Internal Falling in Love

- Ryan's Perspective: Following their intimate moment, Ryan becomes aware that he is genuinely falling for Jessica. He revels in how she brings out parts of him he didn't think existed—a softer, more authentic side. Watching her command the screen and seeing her determination ignites a fire in him to do better—not just for himself, but for her. This realization complicates his earlier motivations to keep their bond strictly professional.

Chapter 11: Dark Moment/Pulling Apart

- Jessica's Perspective: Tensions arise when rumors about their closeness begin circulating in the media. Jessica fears being branded as just another actress in a public romance, leading her to withdraw from Ryan. Feeling conflicted about her growing feelings, she decides to put distance between them, convinced it would protect both their careers. This breaking point shatters the connection they had built, leaving Ryan frustrated and heartbroken.

Chapter 12: Resolution

- Ryan's Perspective: Realizing he can't let her go, Ryan confronts Jessica during the film's final days of shooting. He passionately expresses that their relationship is more than just a fleeting romance, challenging her to acknowledge their connection and embrace vulnerability, both personally and creatively. In a heartfelt moment, he reveals his true self and how she inspires him to become better, urging her to take a leap of faith.

Epilogue: Happy Ever After (HEA)

- Jessica and Ryan's Perspectives: Time jumps forward as the film is released to critical acclaim. Jessica and Ryan stand on the red carpet, hand in hand, celebrating not just their success, but their relationship that has blossomed wonderfully. They publicly address the rumors, confirming their love and commitment to each other. Surrounded by friends, flashing cameras, and joyful fans, they realize that despite their rocky start, fate brought them together, and they are ready to embrace their future as partners in both love and life.

Title: Elevator to Love

Chapter 1: Intro to Heroine - HER POV

Amara Morgan is introduced as a dedicated and ambitious office worker who has always put her career ahead of her personal life. She's passionate about her job but feels stifled in a corporate culture that seems disconnected from her creative aspirations. As she navigates the daily grind, the monotony begins to wear on her, and she yearns for something—or someone—to break the routine.

Chapter 2: Intro to Hero - HIS POV

Alex Reynolds is introduced as a handsome and polished executive, known for his charm and charisma throughout the company. Despite his magnetic presence, he often keeps people at arm's length and maintains an aura of mystery. Readers see glimpses of his life as the son of the billionaire CEO, revealing the pressure he feels to live up to his father's legacy while grappling with his desire for independence.

Chapter 3: Meet Cute - HER POV

Amara's day takes an unexpected turn when she finds herself trapped in the elevator with Alex during a sudden power outage. Initial annoyance turns into surprise as she discovers the executive is not only attractive but also engaging. Their encounter is filled with playful teasing and unexpected warmth, creating an instant connection that leaves both feeling exhilarated.

Chapter 4: Growing Attraction/Getting to Know Each Other - HIS POV

As they wait for help, Alex and Amara delve deeper into conversation. He shares vague details about his role in the company while revealing personal stories that hint at his complexity. At the same time, he can't help but notice Amara's intelligence and passion. His internal thoughts reflect growing admiration and attraction, understanding that there's more to her than meets the eye.

Chapter 5: First Kiss - HER POV

The tension in the elevator reaches a boiling point, culminating in a moment of courage when Amara leans in and kisses Alex. It's an electrifying kiss that leaves her breathless and longing for more. As they pull away, both are dazed by the unexpected turn of events, the thrill of whatever just transpired hanging heavily in the air.

Chapter 6: Her Smell - HIS POV

Back in the office after the power is restored, Alex can't shake off the intoxicating scent of Amara that lingered in the elevator. He's distracted by thoughts of her—her laughter, her smile—while his coworkers tease him about his newfound infatuation. Their playful jabs only heighten his embarrassment but also ignite a deeper interest in her, pushing him to analyze what this attraction means.

Chapter 7: His Taste - HER POV

Later, when Amara confides in her close friend about the kiss, her heart races just at the thought of Alex. She reflects on how the kiss felt electric, unlocking a rush of emotions she hadn't anticipated. Her friend urges her to explore this connection, stirring a mixture of excitement and uncertainty in Amara as she navigates her feelings for the executive.

Chapter 8: Internal Conflict/Resistance to Attraction - HIS POV

Conflicted by the budding attraction, Alex grapples with his feelings for Amara. He's torn between wanting to pursue her and the fear of complications arising due to his family's influence. He recalls the pressure of living up to his father's expectations, leading him to question whether he can let himself fall for her without jeopardizing his career.

Chapter 9: Steamy Hot Intimate Scene - HER POV

After days of chance encounters and stolen glances, Amara and Alex have a spontaneous meeting outside of work, leading to a passionate encounter in a secluded location nearby. Their chemistry boils over, moving from soft, tentative touches to an intense moment that deepens both their emotions and their physical connection. Amara feels liberated and alive, realizing just how deeply she is drawn to him.

Chapter 10: Internal Falling in Love - HIS POV

As Alex spends more time with Amara, he finds himself captivated by her spirit and determination. Small moments—her laughter, her insights—strengthen his feelings. He starts envisioning a future with her, realizing he's willing to confront the pressures of his family for the chance at a relationship that feels real, nourishing, and fulfilling.

Chapter 11: Dark Moment/Pulling Apart - HER POV

Just as their relationship seems to blossom, a miscommunication occurs when Amara overhears a conversation implying that Alex might have been using her to gain insight into a project or as part of his family's agenda. Feeling hurt and betrayed, Amara distances herself from him, wrestling with her feelings and the fear that their romance may have been a façade.

Chapter 12: Resolution - HIS POV

In the aftermath of their fallout, Alex is determined to win Amara back. He confronts her, revealing his vulnerability and explaining the misunderstandings while professing his genuine feelings. He shares how much she means to him, unearthing his fears of familial pressures and the desire to forge his own path apart from the legacy of his last name. Their conversation leads to a rekindling of connection, bridging the gap of misunderstanding and emotional turmoil.

Epilogue with HEA - HER POV

Months later, Amara and Alex are thriving in both their personal and professional lives. They've successfully merged their passions, collaborating on innovative projects that blend creativity with corporate vision. Their relationship flourishes, filled with mutual respect and affection. In a heartfelt moment, Alex surprises Amara with a romantic gesture that symbolizes their journey together, leaving her confident in their future—a perfect ending to their whirlwind romance, filled with laughter, love, and the promise of adventures yet to come.

Title: Best Friend's Wedding

Chapter 1: Intro to Heroine - Lacy's POV

Lacy Bennett is introduced as a vibrant, creative soul who has dedicated her life to her best friend, Mia. With a successful career as a graphic designer that allows her to express herself, she's often found helping others with their plans—whether it's for design projects or, in this case, organizing her best friend's lavish destination wedding. However, beneath her upbeat exterior, Lacy struggles with feelings of inadequacy as she's perpetually single. The upcoming wedding amplifies her insecurities, making her feel like a third wheel amidst all the love surrounding her.

Chapter 2: Intro to Hero - Hudson's POV

Hudson Parrish is a charming and laid-back guy who works in event planning and is known for his magnetic personality. He's always been the reliable best friend to Mia's fiancé, Mark. On the verge of making some big changes in his life, Hudson is ready to embrace newly found freedom—having navigated a year filled with heartbreak and personal growth. While excited to support Mark on his special day, Hudson grapples with his own emotional scars that keep him hesitant about jumping into anything meaningful.

Chapter 3: Meet Cute - Lacy's POV

On the long flight to Santorini, Lacy's anxiety about attending the wedding solo reaches its peak. To alleviate her nerves, she indulges in several drinks, leading her to pass out and drool on the shoulder of the dashing stranger next to her. When she wakes up, mortified, Lacy apologizes profusely, but Hudson takes it all in stride, managing to lighten the mood with his humor. They exchange fleeting but sincere smiles, an unspoken connection flickering to life between them.

Chapter 4: Growing Attraction/Getting to Know Each Other - Hudson's POV

At the wedding festivities, Hudson becomes aware of Lacy's presence as the maid of honor, and their paths keep crossing despite her attempts to avoid him. As the weekend unfolds, Hudson finds himself drawn to Lacy's creative spirit and captivating smile, intrigued by her witty banter and the way she stands out among the crowd. He admires her from afar, respecting her need for space, but cannot shake the urge to get to know her better.

Chapter 5: First Kiss - Lacy's POV

After a series of humorous mishaps and unexpected interactions throughout the wedding weekend, Lacy finds herself caught in a tender moment with Hudson during the wedding rehearsal dinner. Surrounded by the warmth of friends and laughter, Lacy impulsively leans in for a kiss, electrifying and unexpected. The kiss leaves her breathless, awakening feelings she's been too afraid to acknowledge, igniting a spark she never thought she could feel at her best friend's wedding.

Chapter 6: Her Smell - Hudson's POV

As the night goes on, Hudson can't help but replay the memory of Lacy's intoxicating scent in his mind, mixed with jasmine and a hint of citrus—something uniquely her. Every time he brushes past her or their arms accidentally touch, an exhilarating jolt of energy courses through him. He chats with his best friends and can't help but let them tease him about his obvious attraction to Lacy, and there's an undeniable grin on Hudson's face.

Chapter 7: His Taste - Lacy's POV

Later that night, Lacy confides in her sister about the kiss, recalling the sweetness of Hudson's lips and the thrill of it all. As she reflects on their connection, she realizes that this unexpected romance feels profoundly different from anything she's experienced before. Her heart races at the thought of Hudson, making her question her previous intentions of staying away from him.

Chapter 8: Internal Conflict/Resistance to Attraction - Hudson's POV

Despite their undeniable chemistry, Hudson struggles with his internal conflict. He's reminded of his past heartbreak and fears that fully engaging with Lacy might lead to more emotional turmoil. He contemplates whether he can allow himself to love again, contemplating the weight of his emotions amid the festivities of a wedding that shouldn't be about him. Hudson's mind races, caught between wanting to pursue Lacy and the protective mechanisms he instinctively erects.

Chapter 9: Steamy Hot Intimate Scene - Lacy's POV

Caught up in the romance of the wedding weekend, Lacy and Hudson find themselves alone during a sunset walk along the beautiful coastline of Santorini. In a steamy moment filled with longing and passion, they come together in an intimate embrace, leading to a heart-pounding encounter. The warmth of the atmosphere mirrors the electricity between them, igniting a deep connection Lacy had been hesitant to explore fully.

Chapter 10: Internal Falling in Love - Hudson's POV

As the wedding weekend progresses, Hudson realizes that he is falling for Lacy. He reflects on their shared moments of laughter, intimacy, and raw connections. In conversations with Mark and Mia, Hudson begins to open up about his fears of vulnerability, admitting that Lacy makes him want to take a chance on love again. He starts to envision a future filled with creativity, friendship, and romance, solidifying the magnetic bond they've fostered.

Chapter 11: Dark Moment/Pulling Apart - Lacy's POV

Just as Lacy thinks everything is heading in a meaningful direction, a misunderstanding occurs when she overhears Hudson confiding in Mark about his reservations concerning their relationship. Stressed and hurt, she misinterprets his concerns as signs of his wanting to keep their relationship casual. Feeling rejected and ashamed of her own vulnerability, Lacy pulls away from Hudson, opting to return to her guarded demeanor.

Chapter 12: Resolution - Hudson's POV

Realizing the rift that has developed between them, Hudson confronts Lacy, revealing his true feelings and intentions. He clarifies the miscommunication, expressing how deeply he cares for her and his desire to build something lasting. Hudson opens up about his fears of vulnerability but reassures Lacy that she's different, igniting a spark of hope in her heart. Their heartfelt conversation rekindles the flame of connection, bringing them back together at the wedding's closing celebration.

Epilogue with HEA - Lacy's POV

Months later, Lacy and Hudson are thriving in their new relationship, having successfully navigated their fears and chosen to embrace their growing love. They reminisce about the wedding weekend, celebrating milestones together, and planning a future intertwined with creativity and passion. Lacy's heart expands with joy not only for her best friend's marriage but also for her own blossoming love story, knowing she found something profound in the most unexpected moment of her best friend's wedding.

Title: The Stranger

Chapter 1: Intro to Heroine - Ciara's POV

Ciara Thorne is introduced as an adventurous and ambitious young woman living in Munich. She enjoys exploring the city but is often caught up in the responsibilities of her demanding job as a marketing consultant. Despite her professional success, Ciara feels unfulfilled and yearns for spontaneity and excitement in life. We see her in her element—filled with laughter and camaraderie with friends at a local beer garden.

Chapter 2: Intro to Hero - Luca's POV

Luca Rossi is introduced as a free-spirited artist who's traveling across Europe for inspiration. He's a passionate soul, fueled by creativity and an insatiable hunger for new experiences. However, beneath his charming exterior lies a fear of commitment and a reluctance to settle down. He is in the beer garden sketching, capturing moments of life around him, but feels a compulsion to delve deeper into the stories behind his art.

Chapter 3: Meet Cute - Ciara's POV

The atmosphere in the beer garden shifts as Ciara becomes aware of Luca, who's stealing glances at her while diligently sketching. Their first real interaction occurs when he bravely approaches her table, handing over a portrait he drew of her with a playful, Ten euros. She is taken aback by his boldness and the accuracy of the illustration. Driven by curiosity, Ciara flirts back and declares she'll buy it, but only if he joins her for a drink.

Chapter 4: Growing Attraction/Getting to Know Each Other - Luca's POV

As they sit together, Ciara and Luca engage in playful banter and increasingly meaningful conversation. Luca admires Ciara's dynamic personality and how she lights up when discussing her passions. He reveals snippets of his artistic journey, explaining why he travels. Their laughter fills the air as their interest in one another grows, and so does the electricity between them, drawing them closer.

Chapter 5: First Kiss - Ciara's POV

After a lively discussion and a few drinks, Ciara playfully challenges Luca about his thoughts on love and art. The tension builds, and in a spontaneous moment, she leans forward and kisses him, a spark igniting between them. It's sweet, unexpected, and leaves them both breathless as they break apart, eyes wide in awe.

Chapter 6: Her Smell - Luca's POV

Later that evening, as he walks home, Luca can't get Ciara out of his mind. He recalls her intoxicating scent—a blend of citrus and warmth that lingers in his memory, multiplying his desire to be close to her again. Every accidental brush of their hands during their conversation flashes back to him, and he can't help but smile at how wrapped up in her he feels. His friends tease him the next day, observing how he lights up at the mere mention of Ciara.

Chapter 7: His Taste - Ciara's POV

Back at her apartment, Ciara reflects on the kiss, replaying it in her mind. She confides in her best friend, Jill, about how thrilling it felt and how Luca's touch ignited warmth within her. Ciara contemplates how unexpectedly sweet he tasted and how it stirred something long dormant inside her. The thrill of the night makes her giddy, and she realizes that Luca might be exactly what she's been yearning for.

Chapter 8: Internal Conflict/Resistance to Attraction - Luca's POV

After their passionate kiss, Luca feels the weight of his internal struggle. He's immensely attracted to Ciara but is haunted by his fear of commitment and the potential of losing his freedom. While wandering through the city, he questions whether it's worth pursuing something deeper, fearing that falling in love with Ciara might uproot the artistic life he cherishes.

Chapter 9: Steamy Hot Intimate Scene - Ciara's POV

In a quiet, secluded park during another lovely afternoon together, the tension between Ciara and Luca reaches a peak. Their playful laughter gives way to heated glances and lingering touches, leading them to share a passionate, steamy encounter. The intimacy deepens their connection, thrilling Ciara but also stirring her worries about how seriously Luca is taking their newly blooming relationship.

Chapter 10: Internal Falling in Love - Luca's POV

As days pass, Luca finds himself falling harder for Ciara. Brief moments—her laugh, the way she gazes at him, her vitality and passions—become music to his heart. In the midst of creating art and sharing time together, he begins to realize that Ciara brings inspiration in ways he never expected. He fights against his old instincts to run, as he truly wants her in his life.

Chapter 11: Dark Moment/Pulling Apart - Ciara's POV

Just as things seem to be evolving beautifully, Ciara senses Luca's hesitation and reluctance to fully commit. A crucial moment arises when she overhears a conversation that hints at his desire for freedom over a serious relationship. Feeling hurt and rejected, Ciara withdraws from Luca, believing that she misread their connection and that it's better to end things before she gets hurt further.

Chapter 12: Resolution - Luca's POV

Determined not to let Ciara slip away, Luca confronts her about their relationship. He admits his fears of commitment but acknowledges that he doesn't want to lose her. They engage in an emotional conversation where Luca expresses how she has inspired him as both an artist and a person. Ciara, torn, finds solace in his honesty, and they reassess their bond, ready to navigate the complexities of love together.

Epilogue with HEA - Ciara's POV

Months later, Ciara and Luca are thriving in their relationship. Both have grown through their challenges, with Luca demonstrating his commitment and loyalty. Ciara showcases her new projects inspired by their experiences, confidently pursuing her passions, knowing that she is supported by Luca. Together, they explore life as partners—adventurous, creative, and deeply in love, united by the spontaneity that first spiraled their worlds together in that quaint beer garden.

Title: Competing for Your Affection

Chapter 1: Intro to Heroine - Chloe's POV

Chloe Reed is a rising star in the music industry, known for her powerful voice and captivating stage presence. She's a judge on the popular TV singing contest Starbound, where she meets talented contestants and critiques their performances. Despite her success, Chloe feels suffocated by the constant media scrutiny and longs for a genuine connection. She's hesitant to open up to anyone, fearing they'll be drawn into the spotlight and lose their sense of identity.

Chapter 2: Intro to Hero - Jeff's POV

Jeff Ellis is a young singer-songwriter with a dream of making it big. He's always been passionate about music and has been performing in local bars and clubs to hone his craft. Jeff's raw talent and charisma have caught the attention of his friends and family, but he's yet to find his big break. He's determined to make a name for himself in the music industry, no matter what it takes.

Chapter 3: Meet Cute - Jeff's POV

Jeff arrives at the audition for Starbound, nervous but determined. As he takes the stage, he captures Chloe's attention with his charming smile and captivating performance. However, things don't go as planned, and Jeff falters spectacularly during his audition. Despite his embarrassment, he leaves the stage with his head held high, determined to do better next time.

Chapter 4: Growing Attraction/Getting to Know Each Other - Chloe's POV

Chloe is drawn to Jeff's charisma and passion for music. She offers him constructive feedback on his performance, and he takes her advice to heart, impressing her with his dedication and work ethic. As they spend more time together, Chloe finds herself feeling a connection with Jeff that she can't ignore.

Chapter 5: First Kiss - Jeff's POV

As Jeff prepares for his second audition, Chloe offers to mentor him, and they spend more time together. One evening, as they're walking through the park, Jeff turns to Chloe and asks if she'd like to grab a drink with him. She agrees, and they share a romantic dinner, followed by a kiss that leaves them both breathless.

Chapter 6: Her Smell - Chloe's POV

As Chloe thinks about Jeff, she can't help but remember the way he smells - a mix of cologne and fresh laundry that's uniquely his. She finds herself drawn to him even when he's not around, remembering the way he smiles and the way his eyes crinkle at the corners.

Chapter 7: His Taste - Jeff's POV

When Jeff kisses Chloe, he's struck by how good it feels. Her lips are soft and inviting, and her taste is sweet and tangy. He can't get enough of her, and as they pull away from each other, he can feel his heart racing with excitement.

Chapter 8: Internal Conflict/Resistance to Attraction - Chloe's POV

As Chloe and Jeff's relationship deepens, Chloe begins to feel the pressure of keeping their relationship a secret from the media. She's afraid of being scrutinized and losing her reputation, and she starts to pull back from Jeff.

Chapter 9: Steamy Hot Intimate Scene - Jeff's POV

Jeff and Chloe's desire for each other becomes too much to ignore, and they give in to their passion. They share a steamy night together, filled with kisses and caresses.

Chapter 10: Internal Falling in Love - Chloe's POV

As Chloe spends more time with Jeff, she realizes that she's falling deeply in love with him. She loves his kind heart, his passion for music, and his infectious smile.

Chapter 11: Dark Moment/Pulling Apart - Jeff's POV

When a tabloid article surfaces revealing their relationship, Chloe is shocked and hurt. She feels betrayed by Jeff for not telling her about the article before it was published. She pulls away from him, leaving him heartbroken.

Chapter 12: Resolution - Chloe's POV

Chloe realizes that she's been unfair to Jeff and that she needs to communicate better with him. She apologizes for her behavior and explains that she was scared of the media scrutiny. Jeff forgives her, and they work through their issues together.

Epilogue with HEA - Chloe & Jeff's POV

Chloe and Jeff's relationship is stronger than ever. They're open about their love for each other, and they're able to navigate the challenges of fame together. They're living proof that love can conquer all, even in the spotlight.

.

Title: Love Life

Chapter 1: Intro to Heroine - Claire's POV

Claire Bennett, an overworked accountant in a bustling city, struggles with the demands of her job, feeling burnt out and unfulfilled. Despite her success, she longs for excitement and connection outside of her desk job. As she reflects on her life, she realizes that she has put her love life on hold for far too long. A weekend getaway with her girlfriends to a dude ranch seems like the perfect escape.

Chapter 2: Intro to Hero - Dean's POV

Dean Cole, the rugged owner of Silver Trails Ranch, is passionate about preserving his family legacy but is overwhelmed by mounting debts. He spends his days juggling the responsibilities of running the ranch while worrying about its uncertain future. Though he's known for his tough exterior, Dean hides his vulnerability beneath the surface. He's determined to save the ranch, but as the walls close in, he's unsure how he can pull it off.

Chapter 3: Meet Cute - Claire's POV

Claire arrives at the ranch, ready for adventure. When she meets Dean for the first time, she misinterprets his gruff demeanor as standoffish, leading to a humorous yet awkward encounter where she accidentally spills water on him. Their initial interaction is playful, filled with banter that ignites a spark that neither of them expects.

Chapter 4: Growing Attraction/Getting to Know Each Other - Dean's POV

As Claire throws herself into ranch life, helping with chores and getting comfortable in the wide-open spaces, she and Dean find themselves working together more often. They share moments of laughter and camaraderie, slowly stripping away the layers of their guarded personalities. Dean starts to notice Claire's determination and strength, deepening his admiration for her.

Chapter 5: First Kiss - Claire's POV

During a late-night stargazing session, Claire and Dean share an intimate moment as they open up about their dreams and fears. The connection grows palpable, and as the night deepens, they share their first kiss beneath a blanket of stars—a kiss filled with longing and promise that transforms their relationship.

Chapter 6: Her Smell - Dean's POV

After the kiss, Dean can't get Claire out of his mind. He finds himself drawn to her scent—a mix of fresh lavender and the outdoors. Every time he catches a whiff of her, it reminds him of how beautiful she is and how alive he feels when they're together. His ranch hands notice his new infatuation, teasing him about his newfound crush on the city girl.

Chapter 7: His Taste - Claire's POV

After their first kiss, Claire reflects on the experience while confiding in her closest girlfriend. She can't shake the feeling of exhilaration and warmth that Dean's kiss sparked. She recalls the taste of his lips, a blend of warmth and depth that sent butterflies fluttering in her stomach. As Claire considers the growing connection, doubt creeps in.

Chapter 8: Internal Conflict/Resistance to Attraction - Dean's POV

Though he's falling for Claire, Dean struggles with the reality of their different worlds. He's burdened by the ranch's financial troubles and fears that falling in love would only complicate things further. Caught between desire and self-preservation, Dean wrestles with whether he can allow himself to fully commit to Claire when his future is so uncertain.

Chapter 9: Steamy Hot Intimate Scene - Claire's POV

One evening after a long day of work at the ranch, Claire and Dean find themselves alone in the kitchen. Their attraction ignites once more, leading to a passionate and steamy encounter that deepens their bond and solidifies their feelings for one another. They share their vulnerabilities during this intimate moment, creating a connection that transcends physical attraction.

Chapter 10: Internal Falling in Love - Dean's POV

In the days following their intimate moment, Dean realizes he's truly fallen for Claire. It's not just her beauty or vitality, but her strength and compassion that captivates him. He starts to envision a future with her, where they could bridge the gap between their lives. However, uncertainty about the ranch's fate lingers in the back of his mind.

Chapter 11: Dark Moment/Pulling Apart - Claire's POV

Just as Claire begins to find hope for a future with Dean, a crisis hits when a news article is published about the struggling ranch, compelling her to think about her own job and responsibilities. She grapples with the fear of media scrutiny impacting her newfound happiness and ultimately pulls away, convincing herself it's safer to return to her old life.

Chapter 12: Resolution - Dean's POV

Dean, hurt and confused, is determined to show Claire the depth of his feelings. With a renewed sense of purpose, he gathers the courage to confront Claire about their relationship. After a heartfelt declaration of love, he shares his plan to save the ranch, inviting her to be a part of it. They come to an understanding that love is worth fighting for, and they decide to navigate their futures together.

Epilogue with HEA - Claire and Dean's POV

Months later, Claire and Dean stand hand in hand, watching as Silver Trails Ranch begins to flourish again, thanks to their teamwork and the bond they've built. They've embraced both their dreams—Claire has found a way to balance her accounting career while still helping with the ranch, and Dean is revitalizing his legacy with her by his side. With hearts full of love, they share a meaningful kiss, knowing they've created a beautiful life together, one filled with love, adventure, and endless possibilities.

Title: Journey With a Stranger

Chapter 1: Intro to Heroine - Emma's POV

Emma Reynolds is introduced at her bustling city job, preparing for the holidays with excitement and anticipation. We learn about her strong family ties and her tradition of spending Christmas with her parents. As the snowstorm forecast looms, Emma's determination to get home fills her thoughts, emphasizing her sense of responsibility and longing for family warmth.

Chapter 2: Intro to Hero - Lucas's POV

Lucas Hayes is presented as a free-spirited and rugged truck driver. We glimpse into his adventurous life on the road, revealing his struggles with loneliness and how the holiday season reminds him of the family he's distanced himself from. Lucas values spontaneity but harbors a painful past connection with Christmas that makes him hesitant to engage closely with anyone, until fate pushes him into action.

Chapter 3: Meet Cute - Emma's POV

At the airport, amidst a chaotic atmosphere full of frustrated travelers, Emma overhears a group discussing the storm's severity. In that situation of despair, Lucas steps in; his confident demeanor draws her attention. Their first interaction is humorous and filled with tension as he jokes about her predicament while offering help. Although Emma is skeptical about traveling with someone she just met, Lucas's sincerity wins her over.

Chapter 4: Growing Attraction/Getting to Know Each Other - Lucas's POV

On the road, as Emma and Lucas embark on their journey, they share personal stories and laughter, developing a playful rapport. Lucas admires Emma's determination and career ambitions, while she is drawn to his adventurous spirit and charisma. The more they share, the more their chemistry intensifies, sparking a mutual curiosity about each other's lives beyond the surface.

Chapter 5: First Kiss - Emma's POV

During a pit stop at a roadside diner, nerves and excitement take over as they engage in a spirited debate about Christmas traditions. When Lucas playfully leans in to make a point, their faces brush, sparking an electric moment that leads to an impulsive kiss. Emma's heart races as she realizes this isn't just a friendly journey; something deeper is beginning to unfold between them.

Chapter 6: Her Smell - Lucas's POV

Lucas finds himself increasingly enchanted by Emma. He can't help but notice her delightful scent—a mix of pine from her holiday fragrance and the freshness of the open road. When they accidentally brush against each other in the truck, he feels an undeniable spark. His friends tease him through texts, mentioning how infatuated he seems, stirring a mix of embarrassment and affection for Emma.

Chapter 7: His Taste - Emma's POV

After their kiss, Emma confides in her best friend over a phone call, replaying the memorable moment in her mind. She recalls the warmth of Lucas's lips and how it ignited a flurry of butterflies in her stomach. As she speaks, she reflects on the complexity of their situation and how the kiss has forced her to reevaluate their growing connection, feeling both exhilaration and confusion.

Chapter 8: Internal Conflict/Resistance to Attraction - Lucas's POV

As they continue on their journey, Lucas grapples with his feelings for Emma. He's captivated by her but fears that allowing himself to invest emotionally could lead to heartache, especially with the reminder of his past challenges. He is torn between embracing the moment and pushing her away to protect himself from vulnerability, leading to momentary distancing that puts a strain on their growing closeness.

Chapter 9: Steamy Hot Intimate Scene - Emma's POV

After a long day of driving through the storm, they arrive at a cozy lodge where they decide to spend the night. As the weather rages outside, the atmosphere inside turns steamy with lingering glances and playful banter. One thing leads to another, and they share a heated encounter, allowing their emotions and desires to take the lead. Emma's inhibitions melt away as they surrender to the moment.

Chapter 10: Internal Falling in Love - Lucas's POV

Post-encounter, Lucas realizes he is falling for Emma. He admires her resilience, intelligence, and the way she lights up in conversation. As they navigate the snowy landscapes together, he reflects on how she's changed his perspective on life, making him long for a future filled with love rather than just a fleeting adventure. He sees potential beyond their road trip and yearns for something more meaningful.

Chapter 11: Dark Moment/Pulling Apart - Emma's POV

Just as the warmth between them peaks, they encounter a major setback—a breakdown of the truck during the worst of the storm. In the midst of the chaos, Lucas's fear of losing her overwhelms him, leading him to push her away emotionally, citing their differences and the uncertainty of their connection. Heartbroken, Emma feels rejected and begins to doubt their bond as Lucas turns inward, retreating to his defenses.

Chapter 12: Resolution - Lucas's POV

Lucas finally confronts his fears as he watches Emma wrestle with her disappointment. Determined not to lose her, he reaches out to her after a night of reflection. He expresses his vulnerabilities, revealing his fears about love but how he doesn't want to let her go. Emma sees Lucas's true self, which strengthens their bond as they come together, realizing they want to embrace the uncertainty together.

Epilogue with HEA - Emma and Lucas's POV

Several months later, Emma and Lucas have settled into a budding relationship, celebrating Christmas with Emma's family. They toast with joy, exchanging gifts and promising to make their own traditions together. Surrounded by warmth and laughter, they cherish the unexpected journey that brought them to love. As they reflect on that fateful road trip, they realize that, sometimes, the most beautiful endings begin with a leap of faith taken together on the open road.

Outline for Whispers of the Wilderness

Chapter 1: Intro to Heroine (Jana)

Jana is introduced as a passionate adventure guide, with a love for nature and a history of leading eclectic groups into the great outdoors. She relishes the spontaneity of her job, often drawing inspiration from the diverse personalities she encounters. However, she struggles with her dreams of becoming a published author, feeling inadequately prepared and fearful of rejection.

Chapter 2: Intro to Hero (Dale)

Dale Hale, the bestselling author, grapples with the haunting silence of writer's block. Despite his successful past, he feels disconnected from his own narrative and yearns for deeper meaning in his life. Behind the glamorous facade lies self-doubt and restlessness that only grow as deadlines loom closer.

Chapter 3: Meet Cute

When Dale arrives at the base camp for his guided trip, he has a humorous run-in with Jana, who is setting up for a group training session. He accidentally trips over a rope, and Jana catches him, leaving them both flustered. Their contrasting personalities—Jana's free-spirited nature and Dale's brooding intensity—are established.

Chapter 4: Growing Attraction/Getting to Know Each Other

During the first few days of the trip, Jana creates opportunities for the group to bond through team-building activities and challenges that yield hilarious mishaps and unexpected moments. Dale begins to observe Jana's fierce spirit and kindness, while Jana sees glimpses of Dale's vulnerability beneath his aloof exterior. They start sharing personal stories around the campfire, and their connection deepens.

Chapter 5: First Kiss

While navigating a particularly tricky portion of the trail, Dale assists Jana after she takes a minor tumble. In the heat of the moment, they share an electrifying kiss that takes both of them by surprise. The kiss is a beautiful blend of passion and tenderness, and sparks fly, but they pull away, uncertain of what it means.

Chapter 6: Her Smell

During the following days, Dale can't shake the lingering scent of Jana's floral shampoo and the freshness of the forest that trails her. He finds himself lost in thoughts of her beauty, infectious laughter, and reassuring presence. A fellow group member notices Dale's distracted demeanor and playfully teases him about having fallen for the wild woman of the woods.

Chapter 7: His Taste

When Jana reflects on their kiss, she confides in her childhood best friend via video call, struggling with the rush of emotions it stirred within her. Memories of the kiss flood her mind—the softness of his lips and the warmth of his breath. She realizes an undeniable attraction has sparked, but doubts linger about whether Dale could ever reciprocate her feelings fully.

Chapter 8: Internal Conflict/Resistance to Attraction

Dale starts to wallow in confusion, battling the urge to fully embrace his feelings for Jana. He's known for being a solitary artist; allowing someone into his heart feels like a risk he's not ready to take. Jana has her own reservations, feeling unworthy of a man of Dale's stature.

Chapter 9: Steamy Hot Intimate Scene

In a moment of vulnerability while stargazing, Jana and Dale share an intense and passionate night together under the stars. Emphasis on their deep chemistry is underscored by natural beauty and romantic vulnerability—fueled by the wilderness surrounding them.

Chapter 10: Internal Falling in Love

The intimacy they shared prompts both Jana and Dale to reassess their feelings. Dale begins to write again, inspired by their experiences together. Jana feels emboldened and starts penning her own stories, drawing strength from Dale's belief in her. They both find courage in their evolving relationship, feeling profoundly connected to each other.

Chapter 11: Dark Moment/Pulling Apart

Just when things seem to be falling perfectly into place, Dale receives an urgent message about a publishing deal that requires his immediate attention. Feeling torn between his career and his blossoming romance, he withdraws from Jana, inadvertently pushing her away. Jana misinterprets his distance and retreats emotionally, leaving them both heartbroken.

Chapter 12: Resolution

After a period of soul-searching, Dale realizes that he can't let the fear of commitment extinguish the joy Jana brings to his life. He embarks on a journey back to the camp with a newfound determination to confess his feelings. Jana, realizing her power and creativity, decides to confront her fears and be more authentic about herself and her aspirations.

Epilogue with HEA

Several months later, Dale invites Jana to his book launch, where he has dedicated a chapter to the unforgettable journey they experienced together. They look at each other, filled with love and triumph; both have embraced their authentic selves, forged through their time in the wilderness together. As the crowd applauds, Dale takes Jana's hand, solidifying their bond with a promise of many more adventures to come. They share a passionate kiss, surrounded by love and the wilderness whispers that brought them together.

Contemporary Romance ~ Part 2

Outline for Paws for Love

Chapter 1: Intro to Heroine - Casey's POV

Casey Donovan is introduced as a 28-year-old dog walker living in the vibrant city of Maplewood. Her life revolves around her furry clients, which bring her joy and fulfillment. Despite her passion for dogs, Casey has a cynically humorous view of relationships, preferring the company of animals over people. Through her thoughts and interactions with the dogs, we learn about her upbringing, her past heartbreak, and her reluctance to open her heart to anyone.

Chapter 2: Intro to Hero - Ryan's POV

Ryan Marshall, a dashing 30-year-old architect, is introduced juggling his demanding career and the chaos of being a single dog owner to Buster, his flatulent, goofy French bulldog. He is well-liked, friendly, and maintains an easygoing demeanor despite life's pressures. Ryan harbors his own insecurities about dating after being hurt in the past, revealing a relatable side beneath his charming exterior.

Chapter 3: Meet Cute - Casey's POV

Casey's first encounter with Ryan is chaotic and unexpected. While walking Buster, Ryan accidentally collides with Casey as he jogs, creating a comical scene as Buster decides to make a run for it. Casey feels flustered but can't help noticing how handsome Ryan is. Their initial interaction is light-hearted yet awkward, setting the stage for the dynamics of their relationship.

Chapter 4: Growing Attraction/Getting to Know Each Other - Ryan's POV

As Casey continues to walk Buster, their paths cross more often. Ryan begins to join Casey on dog walks, and the two exchange amusing stories about their mishaps with Buster. Ryan's genuine interest in Casey shines through as they share laughter and engage in deeper conversations about their lives, hobbies, and dreams. Ryan starts to feel a pull towards Casey that disrupts his routine, but he enjoys the change.

Chapter 5: First Kiss - Casey's POV

One breezy afternoon, after a particularly amusing episode involving Buster and a park full of squirrels, the atmosphere shifts between Casey and Ryan. As they share a moment of laughter, Casey realizes she's been looking forward to these walks more than she cares to admit. Their flirty banter leads to a spontaneous kiss, catching both off guard. The warm, electric connection leaves Casey breathless, marking a turning point in her feelings toward Ryan.

Chapter 6: Her Smell - Ryan's POV

In the days following the kiss, Ryan becomes more aware of Casey, especially her enchanting scent— a blend of lavender and fresh grass that lingers long after they part. He finds himself daydreaming about her, appreciating her beauty and infectious energy. A close friend notices Ryan's distracted demeanor and teasingly warns him about falling for a girl who walks dogs. Ryan brushes off the tease, secretly contemplating how much he's starting to care for her.

Chapter 7: His Taste - Casey's POV

As Casey reflects on the kiss, she confides in her best friend, who encourages her to pursue what she feels. Casey describes the warmth of Ryan's lips and the thrill of that fleeting yet impactful moment. Along with the giddiness, doubt creeps in; she worries about losing her independence and has lingering fears from her past heartbreaks. Nonetheless, the memory of the kiss stirs an excitement she can't ignore, leading her to the resolve to see where this relationship might lead.

Chapter 8: Internal Conflict/Resistance to Attraction - Ryan's POV

Despite his growing feelings, Ryan grapples with his fears of getting hurt again. Encumbered by past experiences, he often pushes Casey away, questioning whether he's ready to dive deeper into a relationship.

He starts avoiding moments that could make their bond more intimate, trying to maintain a friendly façade while hiding his true emotions. The conflict between wanting to open up and holding back creates tension in their relationship.

Chapter 9: Steamy Hot Intimate Scene - Casey's POV

During an unexpected rainstorm, Casey and Ryan seek refuge in his apartment, bringing Buster along. The atmosphere becomes charged with a mix of laughter and warmth as they dry off. The playful teasing leads to a deeper connection, resulting in a passionate moment where they both give in to their desires. It's an intimate encounter filled with vulnerability, and Casey realizes that she wants more from Ryan than just fun dog walks.

Chapter 10: Internal Falling in Love - Ryan's POV

As Ryan processes the intimate night shared with Casey, he realizes he's falling deeply in love with her. Each encounter further affirms his feelings, from the way she laughs at Buster's antics to how she effortlessly brings joy into his life. Ryan's internal dialogue reveals a longing for not just physical closeness but emotional intimacy as well. He starts crafting plans for a future together, all while grappling with his fears of commitment.

Chapter 11: Dark Moment/Pulling Apart - Casey's POV

After a particularly jovial evening, Casey receives news that she has to move away for a new job opportunity. Panic sets in as she realizes that their budding relationship might be crushed by distance. In a moment of fear, Casey distances herself from Ryan, convincing herself that it's better to cut ties now rather than face potential heartbreak. Her conflicting emotions leave Ryan confused and hurt, marking a drastic turn in their once-flourishing connection.

Chapter 12: Resolution - Ryan's POV

Determined to find Casey before she leaves, Ryan confronts her at the park with Buster. He passionately expresses his feelings and the realization that love is worth the risks. Casey, moved by his earnestness, shares her fears but also admits she doesn't want to lose what they have. Together, they agree to navigate the future, countering doubts with a commitment to make their relationship work, no matter the distance.

Epilogue with HEA - Casey's POV

A year later, Casey and Ryan are thriving together, adapting well to the challenges of long-distance during the week while cherishing weekends filled with dog walks and cozy evenings. Casey feels empowered by her career while knowing that Ryan is beside her every step of the way. Their passionate connection has evolved into a deep, loving relationship full of laughter, Buster-focused adventures, and plans for a life together—a testament to the fact that love can truly be unconditional, whether it's for humans or dogs.

Outline for Driving Him Away

Chapter 1: Intro to Heroine - Ella's POV

Ella Jenkins is introduced as a hardworking single mom navigating the complexities of her life. We delve into her busy routine, balancing her full-time job as an administrative assistant with her part-time job as a waitress. Ella reflects on the struggles she faces trying to provide for her son, Max, and the loneliness she feels, yearning for a personal connection but putting her son first.

Chapter 2: Intro to Hero - Brent's POV

Brent Adderson, a charismatic new manager at Ella's second job, is introduced. He has just relocated to the area with aspirations to climb the corporate ladder and create a positive work environment. Responsible yet laid-back, Brent is a people person who believes in building genuine connections. He reflects on the challenges of being new in town and his excitement about finding love.

Chapter 3: Meet Cute - Ella's POV

Ella and Brent's first encounter occurs at the restaurant where she works. Caught in a rush, she spills coffee all over Brent's crisp shirt while taking an order. Embarrassed yet flustered, they share a laugh amidst the chaos, setting off a spark between them. Their playful banter hints at a connection neither of them expected.

Chapter 4: Growing Attraction/Getting to Know Each Other - Brent's POV

As weeks pass, Brent becomes increasingly interested in Ella. He finds every excuse to interact with her at work, creating opportunities to learn more about her life and her role as a dedicated mother. He is captivated by her strength and resilience while unwittingly becoming attached to little Max, all while feeling the pressure of their complicated dynamic.

Chapter 5: First Kiss - Ella's POV

After a particularly busy shift, Ella and Brent share a quiet moment while closing up the restaurant. Emotions boil over as they share a charged conversation that leads to their first kiss—a blend of nervous energy and longing. Ella is swept off her feet, but the moment is tinged with anxiety as she realizes the implications of getting involved with a man while being a single mom.

Chapter 6: Her Smell - Brent's POV

As Brent thinks about Ella during a rare quiet moment, he becomes aware of the scent of fresh lemon and spring flowers that lingers on her, reminding him of her beauty and the effortless way she brightens his days. He can't help but smile when he recalls her laughter and the way her eyes light up. His best friend, Mark, notices Brent's change in demeanor and starts teasing him about being smitten.

Chapter 7: His Taste - Ella's POV

In the aftermath of their kiss, Ella confides in her close friend Sophie about the experience. The taste of Brent's lips, the closeness, and the warmth send shivers down her spine. While she loves the way he makes her feel, she also feels conflicted, wondering if pursuing him would be selfish as Max seems to disapprove of any new relationship.

Chapter 8: Internal Conflict/Resistance to Attraction - Brent's POV

Brent confronts his feelings for Ella, battling the internal voice that questions whether pursuing her is worth the potential complications. He genuinely likes her and wants to be there for her, but he grapples with the reality that he doesn't want to step on Max's toes. Meanwhile, he worries whether he is stepping into a role he may not be ready for.

Chapter 9: Steamy Hot Intimate Scene - Ella's POV

One night, after a dinner date that starts as a delightful escape but soon escalates, Ella and Brent end up at her apartment. They share a passionate moment that leads to an intense, intimate night together, filled with laughter, tenderness, and a realization of how beautiful their connection has grown. Ella allows herself to enjoy the moment despite the lingering doubts in her mind.

Chapter 10: Internal Falling in Love - Brent's POV

After their intimate encounter, Brent begins to envision a future with Ella and Max. He admires how she balances her responsibilities and starts to feel a burgeoning love for both of them. Brent muses about how delightful Max's antics are and realizes he genuinely cares for Ella, leaving him more determined than ever to make this work despite the odds.

Chapter 11: Dark Moment/Pulling Apart - Ella's POV

The joyful moments turn chaotic when Max confronts Ella about Brent, revealing his disapproval and fears of losing their special bond. Hurtful misunderstandings ensue, leading to an emotional confrontation where Ella, torn between her son's feelings and her relationship with Brent, pushes him away, fearing she may have overstepped her boundaries.

Chapter 12: Resolution - Brent's POV

Brent feels heartbroken but knows he still wants Ella in his life. He reaches out, intent on proving to both Ella and Max that he can be an integral part of their world, not a disruptor. He meets with Max and shares his intentions, letting the boy know he cares about his mom and that he is here to support their little family. They work through their issues with heartfelt discussions, leading to a renewed sense of understanding.

Epilogue with HEA - Ella's POV

Months later, Ella and Brent are happily navigating life together. They have become a cohesive family unit with Max, creating the perfect balance between love, acceptance, and humor. They celebrate Max's achievements, and Brent is embraced wholeheartedly as part of their lives. Ella reflects on how love has blossomed, realizing that they are stronger together than apart, as they embark on new adventures side by side.

Outline for Caught in the Act

Chapter 1: Intro to Heroine - Jessica's POV

Jessica Turner is a spirited and witty thirty-something who pours her soul into her independent bookstore, The Word Nook. She juggles her love of literature with the day-to-day struggles of running a small business. Lately, however, her heart is feeling heavy as a series of break-ins leave her feeling vulnerable. Through her thoughts and interactions with her quirky customers, we get glimpses into her personality, her dreams of romance, and her fears of opening her heart again.

Chapter 2: Intro to Hero - Dalton's POV

Officer Dalton Reynolds, a charming and handsome police officer in his late twenties, is introduced while on patrol in Pinecrest He displays a relatable mix of confidence and self-doubt, trying to prove himself as a reliable officer after a rocky start in his career. He is dedicated to serving his community and is also secretly single, longing for a connection but weary from the rigors of dating in his line of work. Dalton's character is fleshed out through interactions with his colleagues and his reflections on his past relationships.

Chapter 3: Meet Cute - Jessica's POV

Jessica's first official encounter with Officer Dalton is less than conventional. After a particularly chaotic day at the bookstore, Jessica accidentally bumps into him while trying to get a customer's book off a high shelf, causing a hilarious chain reaction that knocks over a display. Dalton comes to her aid, and their banter captures their initial chemistry. Jessica can't help but feel flustered by his easy charm, while Dalton is impressed by her spunky spirit, making it a memorable and awkward first meeting.

Chapter 4: Growing Attraction/Getting to Know Each Other - Dalton's POV

Back at the bookstore for another suspicious alarm, Dalton finds himself engaged in friendly conversation with Jessica. As they share stories, he begins to appreciate her humor, passion for books, and tenacity while helping her assess the security situation. Each visit brings them closer, marked by shared laughter and sidelong glances that highlight their growing attraction. While his instincts as a protector kick in, he finds himself captivated by her vibrant personality.

Chapter 5: First Kiss - Jessica's POV

During a late-night shift at the bookstore, Jessica and Dalton share a moment as they work together to secure the store after another alarm incident. A playful argument escalates into an unexpected kiss fueled by chemistry and frustration. Jessica is left breathless and elated, realizing that this handsome cop has ignited feelings she had buried. Simultaneously, Dalton feels exhilarated yet conflicted about crossing professional lines, leaving both of them questioning the implications of their emotions.

Chapter 6: Her Smell - Dalton's POV

In the days following the kiss, Dalton can't shake thoughts of Jessica. He becomes entranced by her scent—a blend of fresh paper, coffee, and floral perfume—that lingers in his mind long after they part. He catches himself daydreaming about her while on patrol, where his partner and friends tease him about being lovesick. Embarrassed yet undeniably drawn to her, Dalton begins to realize he might be more invested in this relationship than he had intended.

Chapter 7: His Taste - Jessica's POV

Alone and still buzzing from their kiss, Jessica confides in her best friend, Lucy, about her unexpected feelings for Dalton. She describes the warmth and intensity of the kiss, feeling both thrilled and frightened by the connection they share. Lucy encourages her to embrace the romance, while Jessica battles inner doubts, questioning whether she's ready to risk her independence for a relationship. The chapter captures Jessica's blend of excitement and vulnerability.

Chapter 8: Internal Conflict/Resistance to Attraction - Dalton's POV

As their interactions continue, Dalton battles his inner conflict over his emerging feelings for Jessica. Memories of his past heartbreak and fears of complicating his professional life lead him to put up emotional walls. He constantly finds reasons to keep his distance, worried that getting closer could end in disappointment. The chapter dives into Dalton's mind as he grapples with the tension between his heart and his responsibilities.

Chapter 9: Steamy Hot Intimate Scene - Jessica's POV

After a particularly stressful day filled with alarms and a heart-to-heart, Dalton surprises Jessica with a spontaneous dinner date at her favorite restaurant. Their chemistry ignites as they enjoy each other's company, leading to a steamy, passionate reunion at her bookstore afterward. Feeling free from their worries, they lose themselves in each other, creating a tender moment that intensifies their bond and explores the depth of their attraction.

Chapter 10: Internal Falling in Love - Dalton's POV

Post their intimate night, Dalton becomes acutely aware of how profoundly Jessica has entered his heart. He recalls moments from their growing friendship, realizing how she brings a lightness to his life that he never imagined was possible. As he patrols the streets, he begins to visualize a future with her but wrestles with whether he can truly commit, filling the chapter with a mixture of introspection and hope.

Chapter 11: Dark Moment/Pulling Apart - Jessica's POV

Despite their blissful moments, complications arise when Jessica learns of Dalton's hesitation in fully embracing their relationship. Feeling rejected and misunderstood, she decides to step back, believing it's best to protect her heart and her bookstore. Dalton's struggle to articulate his feelings creates a painful misunderstanding as Jessica thinks he's pulled away. A confrontation highlights their fears, leaving an emotional chasm that hinders their ability to communicate and connect.

Chapter 12: Resolution - Dalton's POV

Determined to make things right, Dalton confronts Jessica and admits his fears, revealing that he's fallen for her but was afraid of the risks involved. He explains that his feelings are genuine and that he wants to support her dreams, not detract from them. Moved by his honesty, Jessica allows herself to be vulnerable and shares her feelings as well. Together, they find a way to bridge their emotional divide and create a path forward as a couple.

Epilogue with HEA - Jessica's POV

Several months later, Jessica and Dalton are thriving together, navigating their relationship with humor and partnership. The Word Nook has become a community hub, and with Dalton as her biggest supporter, Jessica feels empowered in both her business and her love life. They reflect on their journey filled with laughter, love, and unexpected challenges. Surrounded by their friends during a community event, Dalton surprises Jessica with a heartfelt gift—a new security system for her bookstore—symbolizing his commitment to both her safety and their budding future. With their hands intertwined and a shared vision, they embrace the promise of many more chapters to come, together.

Outline for Crossing Lines

Chapter 1: Intro to Heroine (Myra's POV)

Meet Myra, a free-spirited artist in her early twenties, living in the city with her brother Nick. She's always been the creative type, with a passion for music and a dream of making it big one day. Myra's independent nature makes her the epitome of a small-town girl with big city dreams. She values her relationships deeply and has a special bond with her brother, Nick.

Chapter 2: Intro to Hero (Ronan's POV)

Ronan Williston is introduced as Nick's best friend, a dependable and fun-loving guy who has a knack for making everyone laugh. He's the glue that holds their group of friends together and is always there for Nick. Ronan has a reputation for being the guy who never gets serious, but deep down, he's hiding a secret - he's tired of his carefree lifestyle and is searching for something more meaningful.

Chapter 3: Meet Cute (Myra's POV)

At a local art show, Myra showcases her talents, and Ronan, being the supportive friend he is, attends to show his support for her. As they catch up, their easy banter and laughter catch the attention of others, but it's a moment of genuine connection between them that sparks something more.

Chapter 4: Growing Attraction/Getting to Know Each Other (Ronan's POV)

Over the next few weeks, Ronan and Myra grow closer as they spend more time together, exploring the city and sharing stories. Ronan finds himself drawn to Myra's creativity and enthusiasm, but he's hesitant to acknowledge his growing feelings, fearing it might ruin his friendship with Nick.

Chapter 5: First Kiss (Myra's POV)

At a rooftop party, under the stars, Ronan and Myra share a moment that changes everything - their first kiss. The chemistry between them is undeniable, and Myra feels like she's found someone who truly understands her.

Chapter 6: Her Smell (Ronan's POV)

As they spend more time together, Ronan becomes fixated on Myra's scent - a unique blend of lavender and vanilla that reminds him of her beauty and her smile. He finds himself thinking about her often, wondering what she's up to and if she's thinking of him too.

Chapter7: His Taste (Myra's POV)

After their magical first kiss, Myra experiences a whirlwind of emotions. Sitting at her art desk, surrounded by her unfinished canvases, she can still taste the lingering sweetness of Ronan's lips—a subtle hint of the peppermint gum he always chews. The memory of that kiss floods her with warmth and excitement, causing her heart to race. As she thinks back to the way he held her face gently in his hands, Myra realizes she's never felt so desired and cherished by anyone before. Confiding in her closest friend, Sophie, she whispers, I can't stop thinking about how his kiss tasted. It was sweet and thrilling... and addictive.

Chapter 8: Internal Conflict/Resistance to Attraction (Ronan's POV)

Despite his growing feelings for Myra, Ronan is torn. He knows that pursuing a relationship with her could jeopardize his friendship with Nick, and he doesn't want to hurt his best friend.

Chapter 9: Steamy Hot Intimate Scene (Myra's POV)

As their relationship deepens, Ronan and Myra share a passionate night together. The chemistry between them is undeniable, and they both know that they're meant to be together.

Chapter 10: Internal Falling in Love (Ronan's POV)

As they navigate their relationship, Ronan realizes that he's falling in love with Myra. He knows that he wants to spend the rest of his life with her, but he's scared to tell her.

Chapter 11: Dark Moment/Pulling Apart (Myra's POV)

When Nick finds out about their relationship, he's upset. He feels like Ronan has betrayed him, and he doesn't know how to deal with it. The tension between the three of them comes to a head, and it seems like their relationship is doomed.

Chapter 12: Resolution (Ronan's POV)

In the end, Ronan realizes that his feelings for Myra are stronger than his friendship with Nick. He knows that he has to choose between the two, and he chooses Myra. They work through their issues and come out stronger on the other side.

Epilogue with HEA (Myra's POV)

In the end, Ronan and Myra realize that their love is worth fighting for. They work through their issues and come out stronger on the other side. They get married in a beautiful ceremony surrounded by their friends and family, including Nick, who has come to accept their relationship.

Outline for Familiar Face

Chapter 1: Intro to Heroine - Lyn's POV

Lyn Torres, a passionate and ambitious chef, reflects on her journey from a humble culinary student to an up-and-coming chef receiving accolades in her city. Despite her success, she feels a lingering loneliness and dreams of owning her own restaurant someday. As she prepares for the Culinary Clash show, her excitement and anxiety bubble to the surface.

Chapter 2: Intro to Hero - Marco's POV

Marco Reyes is introduced as a talented sous chef at a prestigious restaurant, known for his charm and cheeky personality. He feels trapped in his current position and longs to prove himself as a head chef. When he receives the invitation to compete on Culinary Clash, he sees this as his chance to showcase his skills to a broader audience—and perhaps to rekindle some old flames along the way.

Chapter 3: Meet Cute - Lyn's POV

On the set of Culinary Clash, Lyn is thrilled to be in front of the camera but is thrown for a loop when she unexpectedly bumps into Marco in the green room. Their initial surprise morphs into playful banter, reminiscent of their first meeting at the workshop. Lyn's heart races as she remembers their chemistry, yet she tries to maintain a professional demeanor.

Chapter 4: Growing Attraction/Getting to Know Each Other - Marco's POV

As the competition unfolds, Marco is drawn to Lyn's passion for cooking and her determination to succeed. He admires her skills as a chef but is equally intrigued by her humorous personality and zest for life. Through shared challenges—like a team-based round of cooking—they bond over laughter, rivalries, and moments of vulnerability, deepening their connection.

Chapter 5: First Kiss - Lyn's POV

During a particularly high-stress challenge, Lyn and Marco team up for the first time. After successfully completing the task, they steal a moment away from the cameras to celebrate their victory. The chaos of the competition fades away as they share their first kiss, an electrifying moment filled with unspoken longing. They realize that this relationship has become more than just competitiveness; it's a genuine connection.

Chapter 6: Her Smell - Marco's POV

Marco finds himself thinking about Lyn constantly, especially the way her hair smells, like a mix of citrus and herbs from the kitchen.

He remembers the way she looked when she laughed and how vibrant she is, his heart racing each time they accidentally brush against each other while cooking. His coworker, Danny, picks up on Marco's shift in demeanor and playfully nudges him, teasing him about being smitten by Lyn.

Chapter 7: His Taste - Lyn's POV

In her hotel room after a particularly challenging day of competition, Lyn reflects on the kiss with Marco. She confides in her best friend, Sarah, who encourages her to embrace her feelings instead of pushing them away. Lyn feels butterflies each time she thinks about Marco—the way he kissed her left a lasting impression, filling her with a mix of excitement and uncertainty.

Chapter 8: Internal Conflict/Resistance to Attraction - Marco's POV

As they get closer, Marco struggles with his past mistakes that led him to distance himself from Lyn previously. He fears that his growing feelings could distract him from the competition and jeopardize his chance at success. Balancing his ambition with personal emotions becomes increasingly challenging as he grapples with whether he should prioritize their connection or his career.

Chapter 9: Steamy Hot Intimate Scene - Lyn's POV

After a successful elimination round, Lyn invites Marco to her hotel room to celebrate. The atmosphere becomes charged with tension as they cook together, and their chemistry ignites once again. As they prepare dishes and share playful banter, it leads to another passionate kiss that quickly escalates into a steamy intimate encounter. In this moment, they fully embrace their connection, setting aside all reservations.

Chapter 10: Internal Falling in Love - Marco's POV

Post-intimacy, Marco feels his walls coming down as love blossoms within him. He admires Lyn's creativity, her compassion, and how she fiercely fights for her dreams. He begins to imagine a future with her—one where they might collaborate in their culinary adventures. Yet, he still grapples with the fear that their relationship could complicate their professional lives.

Chapter 11: Dark Moment/Pulling Apart - Lyn's POV

Unforeseen drama unfolds when a twist in the competition puts pressure on both cooks. Marco receives a lucrative job offer that could take him away right after the show, sparking worries that Lyn could lose him yet again. When Lyn's insecurities bubble to the surface, she feels unworthy of Marco's affections, ultimately leading to a heated argument about their priorities. Both retreat emotionally, leaving their relationship in jeopardy.

Chapter 12: Resolution - Marco's POV

Marco realizes that his feelings for Lyn are more important than a temporary job opportunity, and he wants to fight for their relationship. He confronts Lyn, expressing his intent to pursue both culinary excellence and love. They talk through their fears and misunderstandings, resolving to support each other's dreams while navigating their budding romance together. They both agree that love can fuel ambition, not detract from it.

Epilogue with HEA - Lyn's POV

Several months later, Lyn opens the doors to her dream restaurant, which prominently features a menu inspired by both her and Marco's culinary styles. As she stands proudly in her new establishment, Marco enters, their eyes locking in an unspoken promise. The episode that once complicated their lives has become a cornerstone of their bond. They celebrate their successes—individually and as a couple—recognizing that together, they have created a new recipe for happiness rooted in love, ambition, and mutual support.

Title: Love On the Way Up

Chapter 1: Intro to Heroine - Reylie's POV

Reylie Bennett is a driven and ambitious marketing consultant in her late twenties, determined to make her mark in the competitive world of Manhattan's business landscape. We see glimpses of her daily life, filled with deadlines and demanding clients, but also witness her quiet longing for deeper connections. As she prepares for an important pitch meeting at the Chrysler Building, she grapples with self-doubt and the fear of failing to live up to her potential.

Chapter 2: Intro to Hero - Evan's POV

Evan Sinclair, an equally ambitious entrepreneur in his early thirties, is introduced as a man with charm, intelligence, and a polished exterior. He's focused on launching his new tech startup but feels frustrated with the superficial connections in his life. Passionate about innovation and making an impact, Evan is also searching for something meaningful. As he heads to a meeting that could change his career, he reflects on his past and what he's looking for in life.

Chapter 3: Meet Cute - Reylie's POV

Reylie enters the elevator and immediately notices Evan. He stands out among the sea of suits, exuding confidence and style. As the elevator doors close, she feels a spark of attraction but struggles to think of a way to start a conversation. Instead, they exchange polite yet unengaged glances, filling the ride with an air of expectancy. Just as the elevator begins to ascend, the lights flicker.

Chapter 4: Growing Attraction/Getting to Know Each Other - Evan's POV

When the blackout plunges them into darkness and stops the elevator, Evan's initial surprise transforms into an opportunity to connect. He breaks the silence by speaking up, joking about how they've now become elevator buddies. They share stories in the dim light, learning about their dreams and ambitions while feeling the intensity of their attraction grow. Evan finds himself captivated by Reylie's wit, while she admires his charisma and intelligence.

Chapter 5: First Kiss - Reylie's POV

After several minutes of laughter and shared vulnerability, Reylie and Evan's conversation deepens, revealing their fears and aspirations. The darkness feels intimate as they inch closer, the chemistry undeniable. Suddenly, in a moment charged with emotion, Evan leans in and kisses her softly but passionately, igniting a spark that leaves Reylie reeling with both exhilaration and confusion.

Chapter 6: Her Smell - Evan's POV

As the power returns and the elevator lurches back to life, Evan can't shake the memory of Reylie's enchanting scent—a mix of citrus and floral notes that lingered in the air. He reflects on her beauty and the way her laughter echoed in the confined space, realizing he is smitten. His coworker notices his distracted demeanor and teases him playfully about the mysterious woman from the elevator, prompting Evan to blush and brush off the comment while secretly yearning for more.

Chapter 7: His Taste - Reylie's POV

Later that day, as Reylie sits with her best friend, she recounts the kiss, replaying the soft warmth of Evan's lips against hers. She's both exhilarated and terrified, caught between wanting to explore this connection and fearing it might complicate her already hectic life. Sharing every detail, she confesses how incredible it felt while her friend encourages her to embrace this unexpected chance at happiness.

Chapter 8: Internal Conflict/Resistance to Attraction - Evan's POV

Despite their undeniable chemistry, Evan's past relationships haunt him. He wrestles with fears of vulnerability and the possibility of getting hurt again. He is swept up in curiosity about Reylie, yet is unsure if he's ready to commit to anything serious. As he returns to work, he struggles to focus, realizing how much he desires to see her again, but questioning whether he should take that leap.

Chapter 9: Steamy Hot Intimate Scene - Reylie's POV

After a few days of exchanging texts, Reylie and Evan decide to meet for dinner. The chemistry between them is electric, and as the tension mounts, they find themselves drawn to one another in a quiet corner of the restaurant. This time, their kiss is fueled with passion and urgency, leading to an intimate moment that feels like the culmination of their connection and shared experiences.

Chapter 10: Internal Falling in Love - Evan's POV

As their relationship develops, Evan becomes increasingly aware that he is falling for Reylie. He admires her ambition and unwavering spirit, and every small moment they share deepens his affection. Yet, he's conflicted, torn between his desire for love and the fear of failure. He grapples with the reality of a relationship blossoming while maintaining his career ambitions.

Chapter 11: Dark Moment/Pulling Apart - Reylie's POV

Amid the growing love, unforeseen challenges arise when Evan misses one of Reylie's important events due to a business commitment. Reylie, feeling neglected and insecure, doubts whether Evan truly cares or if he is just another fleeting connection. Conflicted and hurt, she decides to take a step back, leading to an emotional confrontation that leaves them both shattered and questioning their relationship.

Chapter 12: Resolution - Evan's POV

Determined to make things right, Evan reaches out to Reylie, pouring his heart out and explaining how much she means to him. He acknowledges his mistakes and demonstrates the sincerity of his feelings. Their conversation leads to a powerful realization: Love is worth the risk, and they both want to navigate these challenges together. They decide to work through their fears, excited for what the future might hold.

Epilogue with HEA - Reylie and Evan's POV

Months later, Reylie and Evan are seen thriving in both their careers and relationship. They visit the Chrysler Building, reminiscing about the fateful elevator ride that brought them together. They embrace the adventure of building a life as partners, each supporting the other's dreams while reflecting on how far they've come. As they gaze out at the breathtaking New York skyline, hand in hand, they look forward to a future filled with endless possibilities, solidifying their love story as one of serendipity and connection.

Outline for Stuck at the Top
Chapter 1: Intro to Heroine (Mia's POV)

Mia Thompson is introduced as a passionate and ambitious journalist in her late twenties who thrives on getting the perfect story. She struggles with feelings of inadequacy and the pressure to succeed in a competitive industry. Her latest assignment is to cover the local county fair, but she views it as just another task to navigate rather than an adventure. As she reflects on her childhood memories of fairs, Mia tries to rekindle her excitement but is overwhelmed by her own expectations.

Chapter 2: Intro to Hero (Jake's POV)

Jake Rivers is introduced as a free-spirited photographer in his early thirties who finds beauty in the mundane and captures life's fleeting moments. He thrives on spontaneity and adventure but is haunted by a recent breakup that has left him questioning his long-term goals. While he admires his friends' settled lives, he enjoys fleeting connections. As the fair approaches, he reflects on how photography is his true love, and hopes to find a spark of inspiration in the familiar setting.

Chapter 3: Meet Cute (Mia's POV)

Mia's day at the county fair takes a comedic turn when she decides to ride the iconic Ferris wheel for aerial shots, determined to find ways to spice up her article. Unexpectedly, Jake hops into the seat beside her, charmingly haphazard and bursting with humor about carnival cliché. Just as they share a laugh, the Ferris wheel grinds to a halt, trapping them at the top. This initial mishap sets the scene for their first meaningful conversation, mingling laughter and annoyance.

Chapter 4: Growing Attraction/Getting to Know Each Other (Jake's POV)

With the Ferris wheel creaking in the background, Jake tries to ease the tension and starts sharing amusing fair anecdotes, showcasing his wit and laid-back nature. As they talk, he becomes entranced by Mia's sharp intellect and determination. They discuss their careers and desires, and through their contrasting life perspectives, they discover unexpected commonalities. The attraction builds as they navigate their fears while hanging precariously above the fairground and slowly realizing they enjoy each other's company.

Chapter 5: First Kiss (Mia's POV)

As the sun begins to set, casting a warm glow on them, Mia feels the atmosphere shift. Their playful banter transitions into deeper, more intimate conversations. Feeling a rush of boldness, and drawing closer, Mia leans in and steals a soft, tentative kiss from Jake. It ignites a spark, and the world below fades away as they share the moment, leaving them both breathless and craving more—understanding that what they've just shared is something special.

Chapter 6: Her Smell (Jake's POV)

After their kiss, Jake finds his thoughts consumed by Mia. He becomes hyper-aware of her presence—how her laughter dances in the air and how a hint of lavender lingers around her. Their chemistry is palpable, and during a casual outing afterward, one of Jake's friends jokingly comments on how enchanted he seems by the Ferris wheel girl. Flustered yet exhilarated, Jake can't help but grin, acknowledging to himself that he's falling hard for Mia.

Chapter 7: His Taste (Mia's POV)

Later, as Mia talks with her best friend over coffee, she can't stop replaying their kiss in her mind. She confides how Jake's lips were sweet and tasted of warmth, leaving her with butterflies in her stomach. With a mix of excitement and anxiety, Mia reflects on her growing feelings, grappling with a sense of vulnerability she hasn't felt in a long time. Her friend encourages her to explore this connection, heightened with caution as Mia values her heart too much to risk a casual fling.

Chapter 8: Internal Conflict/Resistance to Attraction (Jake's POV)

Though Jake is buoyed by the connection, he wrestles with his fears of commitment. Memories of his failed relationships claw at him, urging him to pull back. He starts to create emotional distance, convincing himself that it's the safer choice, despite the magnetic pull he feels towards Mia. A chance encounter with an old friend only reinforces his reluctance to dive into something deeper, leaving him torn between attraction and fear.

Chapter 9: Steamy Hot Intimate Scene (Mia's POV)

After an exhilarating day at the fair where sparks ignite between them again, they return to the quieter surroundings of the Ferris wheel at night. Mia and Jake become lost in each other's eyes, sharing a heated kiss that escalates into something much deeper. In the warmth of their intimacy, they explore their passions, creating a whirlwind of shared laughter, whispers, and desire. It's a moment that brings raw emotions to the surface, confirming their undeniable chemistry.

Chapter 10: Internal Falling in Love (Jake's POV)

As the magic of the fair continues, Jake's walls begin to crumble. He realizes that being with Mia makes him the happiest he's ever been. During a quiet walk under twinkling lights, he starts to imagine a future with her—a stark contrast to his traditional notion of love. The simple moments they share—laughter, glances, and flavors of normalcy—become his inspiration, making every captured moment feel profoundly beautiful, all thanks to Mia.

Chapter 11: Dark Moment/Pulling Apart (Mia's POV)

Just when she starts to embrace her feelings for Jake, a journalist from Mia's workplace arrives for the closing fair and inadvertently brings attention to how the fair article was her last distraction. Overhearing a patronize conversation that hints at her unprofessionalism, Mia feels wounded. She wrestles with the idea that her budding romance with Jake could jeopardize her career, prompting her to pull away from him emotionally, creating a rift in their connection.

Chapter 12: Resolution (Jake's POV)

Sensing Mia's withdrawal, Jake resolves to confront his feelings. He finds Mia at the fair just as it's beginning to wind down. In a heartfelt and vulnerable conversation, he expresses how much she means to him, affirming that what they shared was not just a fling but a deep connection. He reassures her that love and passion aren't at odds with ambition, and they both need to take the leap together. In an emotional reunion, they decide to trust each other and the potential for what's to come.

Epilogue: HEA (Mia's POV)

Months later, Mia's article on the fair is published, showcasing not only its charm but the transformative journey she experienced. She and Jake are firmly in a loving relationship, collaborating on creative projects seamlessly and balancing their careers and passions. At the next county fair, they return together, joyous and in love, riding the Ferris wheel once more, sharing laughter, nostalgia, and dreams for their future—under the twinkling starlit sky, embracing every moment together.

Outline for Behind the Velvet Ropes

Chapter 1: Intro to Heroine - Riley's POV

Riley Clark is introduced as a hardworking single mother juggling her waitressing job at a nightclub and caring for her young daughter, Lily. Despite the laid-back glamour of her job, Riley feels the weight of life's struggles, grappling with financial stress and the loneliness of parenthood. We get a glimpse of her disdain for affluent clientele and her determination to provide a better life for Lily, emphasizing her resilience and independence.

Chapter 2: Intro to Hero - Wyatt's POV

Wyatt Reynolds is introduced as the charming, charismatic owner of the nightclub. Behind his easy smile and confident demeanor lies a man haunted by his past—his reputation as a party boy continues to follow him, making genuine connections difficult. We see glimpses of his loneliness, even within the lap of luxury, and an unquenchable desire to change his life and be better than the wild persona the world knows.

Chapter 3: Meet Cute - Riley's POV

During a particularly busy shift, Riley serves a table of rowdy patrons. The atmosphere is chaotic, and she's on edge. Suddenly, she overhears Wyatt having a witty exchange with friends at the bar. When a drink is spilled on her, Wyatt steps in to help, easing her frustration with a simple, charming apology. Their playful banter ignites an instant connection, leaving Riley flustered yet intrigued.

Chapter 4: Growing Attraction/Getting to Know Each Other - Wyatt's POV

Wyatt returns to the club, eager to see Riley again. Their dynamic grows stronger as he engages her in longer conversations after hours, learning about her life, her dreams, and her daughter. Riley is surprised by Wyatt's genuine interest and his kindness, finding herself warming to a man she believed was just another entitled rich kid. Wyatt's admiration for Riley blossoms as he sees her tough exterior yield to her tenderness.

Chapter 5: First Kiss - Riley's POV

After a particularly meaningful night out with Wyatt, where they discuss their hopes and dreams, the chemistry between them reaches a peak. In a stolen moment outside the club, Wyatt leans in, and their first kiss ignites a spark of passion. It's innocent yet charged with desire, leaving Riley breathless and questioning everything she thought she knew about Wyatt.

Chapter 6: Her Smell - Wyatt's POV

Wyatt can't get Riley out of his head. Her unique scent—citrus and a hint of vanilla—lingers with him long after their kiss. In a private moment, he reflects on how she captivates him with her warmth and authenticity. A close friend teases him about his obvious crush, pushing Wyatt to confront his deepening feelings for Riley. Wyatt realizes she is unlike any other woman he's dated.

Chapter 7: His Taste - Riley's POV

Back home, Riley plays the kiss over in her mind, savoring the taste of Wyatt's lips—rich and inviting. She confides in her friend about the kiss, sharing her conflicting feelings about him being the club owner she has openly resented. Their conversation leads her to recognize the complexity of her emotions; she is both drawn and terrified by the idea of falling for someone like Wyatt.

Chapter 8: Internal Conflict/Resistance to Attraction - Wyatt's POV

Wyatt grapples with his dual identity: the carefree party boy the world knows and the man he wants to become for Riley. He battles with fear that his past will overshadow any chance of having a future with her. Torn between his desire for her and his desire to prove he's changed, Wyatt's internal conflict escalates, threatening to drive him away from the one person who truly sees him.

Chapter 9: Steamy Hot Intimate Scene - Riley's POV

After a night out at the club, sparking a deep connection, Wyatt and Riley find themselves in Wyatt's luxurious apartment. Their chemistry explodes into a passionate and steamy encounter that seals their bond. Riley's walls come tumbling down as they explore their intimacy, letting go of their worries for the night. It deepens their connection and sparks new feelings.

Chapter 10: Internal Falling in Love - Wyatt's POV

As Wyatt navigates his growing feelings for Riley, he recognizes that he is truly in love with her. Moments with Lily show him what family means, stirring a desire to leave his old life behind. He dreams of building a future with Riley, one filled with real connection, warmth, and love. Yet, he fears what might happen if they face the judgment of society together.

Chapter 11: Dark Moment/Pulling Apart - Riley's POV

After a glamorous charity event where Wyatt is thrust into the limelight, Riley overhears a hurtful comment about her being just another conquest for Wyatt. Hurt and feeling like she's just one of many, she confronts Wyatt about his past and their differences. The argument escalates, leading to a heartbreaking fallout where Riley decides to pull away, fearing that their worlds are too different to merge.

Chapter 12: Resolution - Wyatt's POV

Realizing the gravity of their separation, Wyatt fights to win Riley back, motivated by love. He declares his long standing desire to change and how profoundly she and Lily have affected him. He takes action, demonstrating his commitment by volunteering at a local charity—exposing the world to his genuine intentions and heartfelt transformation. The moment Riley sees him at the charity event, surrounded by children and exuding authenticity, she is finally swayed.

Epilogue with HEA - Riley's POV

Months later, Riley and Wyatt are happily intertwined in life. Wyatt has proven himself to be a supportive partner and a loving figure for Lily. They attend family gatherings, enjoying blissful moments and building lasting memories. Riley reflects on how far they've come, acknowledging that love and trust have the power to conquer past mistakes. With hearts united, they explore the future together, ready to embrace whatever comes next—truly a family at last.

Outline for Isle of Survival

Chapter 1: Intro to Heroine (Leesa's POV)

Leesa Harris, a passionate marine biologist, is introduced. She's on a small sailing trip to study sea life for an upcoming research project. Despite her adventurous spirit, she struggles with self-doubt, often feeling overshadowed by her peers in a male-dominated field. Leesa dreams of making a groundbreaking discovery but wrestles with the fear that her dreams might remain unfulfilled.

Chapter 2: Intro to Hero (Hunter's POV)

Hunter Thompson, an ambitious and skilled architect, is introduced. He is known for his designs and his ambitious work ethic, but beneath his confident exterior lies a profound fear of failure and the disappointment of his family. Hunter's decision to take a break through sailing was an attempt to clear his head and gain perspective, but he too has personal struggles that haunt him.

Chapter 3: Meet Cute (Leesa's POV)

The boat capsizes in a storm, and as Leesa swims for her life, she collides with Hunter, who is desperately trying to stay afloat. They end up on the same makeshift raft, overwhelmed by fear and the chaotic aftermath of the crash. Amid the panic, their eyes meet, sparking an initial awareness of each other's presence—both intimidating and strangely calming in the madness.

Chapter 4: Growing Attraction/Getting to Know Each Other (Hunter's POV)

As they find their way to the deserted island, Hunter realizes they need to work together for survival. He learns of Leesa's background in marine biology and her ability to identify edible plants and animals. Hunter is captivated by her intelligence and strength as they forage for food and build shelter. Their conversations grow longer and deeper, revealing their hopes and insecurities.

Chapter 5: First Kiss (Leesa's POV)

After days spent overcoming everyday challenges, they sit by a fire one evening, recounting their tales. The chemistry between them is electric, and in a spontaneous moment, they lean in and share a tentative but passionate kiss under the stars. Leesa is exhilarated but uncertain about what it means for their survival situation.

Chapter 6: Her Smell (Hunter's POV)

Hunter becomes acutely aware of Leesa's scent—a mix of saltwater and a hint of coconut from her sunscreen—every time he is near her. Whenever they accidentally brush against each other while gathering wood or preparing food, he feels a rush of something he can't name. A moment shared with a fellow survivor after they make a fire has Hunter's friend teasing him about the island romance, which leaves him flustered but secretly pleased.

Chapter 7: His Taste (Leesa's POV)

After the kiss, Leesa confides in a journal she keeps on the island. Memories of Hunter's kiss linger on her lips, and she's filled with confusion about emotions she didn't expect. She shares her excitement and trepidation with her best friend via text on her satellite phone (which is still functioning, but has limited battery life). Will their potential relationship compromise their survival?

Chapter 8: Internal Conflict/Resistance to Attraction (Hunter's POV)

Despite his growing feelings for Leesa, Hunter wrestles with the line between their survival partnership and a romantic relationship. He fears that letting his emotions get involved could cloud his judgment and endanger their living situation. His internal battle becomes more intense as he finds himself daydreaming about what life could be like with her beyond the island.

Chapter 9: Steamy Hot Intimate Scene (Leesa's POV)

One evening, after gathering food and building a more substantial shelter, the tension culminates in a heat-driven moment, and they surrender to their passion. With the moonlit ocean crashing at their feet, they share a steamy encounter that solidifies their emotional bond, igniting feelings that were merely simmering before.

Chapter 10: Internal Falling in Love (Hunter's POV)

As days turn into weeks on the island, Hunter finds himself falling deeply in love with Leesa. Every shared experience strengthens his affection, from cooking meals together to exploring the beauty of their surroundings. He's captivated by her compassion, intelligence, and adventurous soul, realizing he doesn't just want her as a partner for survival—he wants her in his life forever.

Chapter 11: Dark Moment/Pulling Apart (Leesa's POV)

Just when it seems that rescue is right around the corner, a miscommunication leaves Leesa feeling betrayed over an important decision Hunter makes without consulting her. Overwhelmed by emotions and fear of returning to their old lives, she withdraws and refuses to listen to Hunter's explanations. Hurt words are exchanged, leading to a rift that threatens to unravel their connection and hopes for rescue.

Chapter 12: Resolution (Hunter's POV)

With an impending storm approaching, Hunter realizes they need to reconcile for the sake of survival. He bravely confronts Leesa, pouring out his feelings while acknowledging the risks they both face. He emphasizes that they are stronger together and offers a plan to signal for help. Their shared vulnerability brings them back together, rekindling hope and unity as they weather the storm.

Epilogue: HEA (Leesa's POV)

Months later, Leesa and Hunter are safely back home, forever changed by their experience. They reflect on the bond they forged on the island and how they've decided to pursue their professional dreams in a way that embraces their love for each other. The journey together, once born from necessity, has turned into a partnership anchored in love, respect, and shared experiences. As they walk along the beach where they first met, they vow to support each other's dreams, ready to face whatever the future holds—together.

.

Title: Wanderlust in the Alps

Chapter 1: Intro to Heroine - Jenna's POV

Jenna Thomason is introduced as a recent college graduate determined to find herself after a tough breakup. She reflects on her past relationship while packing her backpack for her European adventure, feeling both excited and apprehensive about her decision to travel solo. Jenna's desire for independence is palpable, along with a hint of vulnerability as she vows to focus on self-discovery.

Chapter 2: Intro to Hero - Luca's POV

Luca Rossi, a mountain guide in his early thirties, is introduced as a ruggedly handsome and carefree spirit. He is well-respected in his community and deeply connected to the land he loves. While he enjoys his work and the adventures it brings, he carries the weight of a failed romance that still lingers in his heart. His passion for guiding people through the beauty of the Italian Alps is evident, alongside an underlying sense of longing.

Chapter 3: Meet Cute - Jenna's POV

Jenna arrives at a quaint mountain lodge where her hiking trip is set to begin. Feeling overwhelmingly out of place amidst seasoned hikers, she accidentally spills her water bottle on Luca while introducing herself. With a smile, he helps her clean up, and their banter flows effortlessly, igniting an unexpected spark. Jenna is immediately intrigued, though she resolves to keep things platonic.

Chapter 4: Growing Attraction/Getting to Know Each Other - Luca's POV

As they embark on their hiking journey through the Alps, Jenna and Luca begin to bond over shared adventures and personal stories. Luca admires Jenna's tenacity and her willingness to explore the mountains. He finds himself drawn to her warmth and vitality, while

Jenna feels a growing comfort around Luca that makes her forget her past. Their chemistry flourishes as they navigate rocky paths and engage in playful teasing.

Chapter 5: First Kiss - Jenna's POV

After a long day of trekking and a breathtaking sunset overlooking the mountains, Jenna and Luca find themselves alone by a serene lake. As they share their hopes and dreams beneath the stars, their conversation turns heartfelt, and a palpable tension builds. Overcome by a surge of emotion, they share their first kiss—soft, tentative, and electric. Jenna feels an exhilarating mix of confusion and excitement as this moment stirs feelings she thought she had buried.

Chapter 6: Her Smell - Luca's POV

Luca is captivated by Jenna's unique scent—a blend of fresh pine and citrus, which reminds him of the beauty surrounding them. As they hike together, he's increasingly aware of how close they are and the warmth that radiates when they accidentally touch. His friends notice his infatuation during the next break, teasing him about his obvious crush on Jenna, and he finds himself unable to deny the truth of their connection.

Chapter 7: His Taste - Jenna's POV

After their kiss, Jenna retreats to her room that night, her heart racing with thoughts of Luca. She shares her mixed feelings with her sister on a video call, recounting the kiss in awe and disbelief. With vivid memories of the warmth of his lips and the impact of that moment, Jenna grapples with self-doubt, uncertain if she's ready to let herself be vulnerable again.

Chapter 8: Internal Conflict/Resistance to Attraction - Luca's POV

Despite his growing feelings for Jenna, Luca wrestles with the fear of falling too hard. Memories of his past relationship haunt him, and he doubts if he should allow himself to become emotionally attached again. He attempts to maintain his distance, though he aches to be close to her, leading to moments of internal anguish and a struggle between his heart and his head.

Chapter 9: Steamy Hot Intimate Scene - Jenna's POV

During a thunderstorm while seeking shelter in a cozy mountain cabin, shared laughter quickly transforms into an intimate moment. The air is charged with unspoken desire, and before she realizes it, Jenna finds herself tangled with Luca on the floor. Their kiss ignites once more, leading to a passionate and steamy encounter that leaves them breathless, yet complicated emotions linger in the air afterward.

Chapter 10: Internal Falling in Love - Luca's POV

As their hiking trip progresses, Luca finds himself increasingly enchanted by Jenna. He watches her face light up during their adventures and admires her courage to push boundaries. With every shared laugh and moment spent in her company, he recognizes that he is falling deeply in love with her, but he remains conflicted. The thought of yet another potential heartbreak looms over him.

Chapter 11: Dark Moment/Pulling Apart - Jenna's POV

Just as they embrace their feelings, Jenna learns that their hiking trip is nearing its end, and Luca hints he may have to return to his life, potentially pulling away from the connection they've built. Afraid of getting hurt again, she decides to put distance between them, leading to a confrontation where they express their fears. Misunderstandings arise, and Jenna pulls back, convinced it's better to remain friends than risk heartbreak.

Chapter 12: Resolution - Luca's POV

Determined to resolve the tension, Luca plans a final adventure. He takes Jenna to a breathtaking viewpoint to confess his feelings, knowing he must fight for her heart. In a poignant moment, he tells her that they could create something beautiful together if they're willing to take the leap. Jenna realizes that her fears are holding her back, and with newfound clarity, she embraces her heart's desire.

Epilogue with HEA - Jenna and Luca's POV

Several months later, Jenna returns to the Alps, this time not just as a hiker but as someone ready to embrace love. Luca meets her with open arms, and together they reminisce about their summer and the breakthroughs they achieved. Hand in hand, they wander through the landscapes where it all began, vowing to navigate life's adventures together. Surrounded by the awe of the mountains, they pledge their hearts, embarking on a new journey filled with love, understanding, and endless exploration.

Outline for Reflections of the Heart

Chapter 1: Intro to Heroine - Amelia's POV

Amelia Rodriguez is introduced as a passionate hairstylist in Hollywood. While she loves her job and the creativity it allows, Amelia often feels alienated by her clients' vanity and superficial concerns. We see her juggling work and supporting her family back home, revealing her dedication and longing for a fulfilling personal life outside of the salon. A glimpse into her past shows the sparks of her dreams and aspirations still flickering, despite her current reality.

Chapter 2: Intro to Hero - Richard's POV

Richard Donovan, a billionaire with a sharp mind and charming demeanor, is revealed through his internal struggles with aging and self-image. Behind his wealth and good looks is a man grappling with insecurities that most people wouldn't guess he harbors. Richard reflects on his past relationships and successes, showing how his focus on pleasing others and maintaining a polished exterior has led him to feel increasingly lonely. The contrast between his public persona and private thoughts is captivating.

Chapter 3: Meet Cute - Amelia's POV

Amelia is busy at work when Richard enters the salon for his weekly appointment. Their introduction is marked by Richard's usual grumpy demeanor, but Amelia, unafraid, calls him out on his obsession with his appearance. Their verbal sparring and banter are laden with tension as Amelia's straightforward nature surprises Richard and helps break the ice. Despite their differences, a strange attraction sparks between them.

Chapter 4: Growing Attraction/Getting to Know Each Other - Richard's POV

As their appointments continue, Richard and Amelia bond over shared interests beyond their professional roles. Richard begins to appreciate Amelia's authenticity, her passion for her work, and her down-to-earth personality. He starts looking forward to their conversations, finding comfort in her laughter and light-heartedness. Through shared stories and candid discussions, they discover common ground, making them both question their preconceived notions about each other.

Chapter 5: First Kiss - Amelia's POV

After a particularly deep conversation about insecurities, Amelia and Richard's chemistry reaches a boiling point. During a light-hearted moment, they lean in, and a spontaneous kiss occurs, electric and intoxicating. Amelia feels both exhilaration and confusion as she processes how different he is from her expectations. The kiss leaves her longing for more but uncertain about where it will lead.

Chapter 6: Her Smell - Richard's POV

After their kiss, Richard can't help but think about Amelia. The scent of her—like fresh flowers mixed with a hint of vanilla—overwhelms him whenever he thinks of her. In a casual conversation with his best friend, Jake, Richard realizes just how smitten he is by Amelia. Jake teases him about his crush, prompting Richard to confront his feelings while he both revels in the warmth Amelia brings into his life and wrestles with his insecurities.

Chapter 7: His Taste - Amelia's POV

Amelia reflects on their kiss in her apartment, savoring the taste of Richard's lips—rich and warm—as she struggles to contain her fluttering emotions. She confides in her close friend, Carla, discussing her fears regarding the budding relationship given their age difference and Richard's social standing. Carla reassures her, emphasizing that their connection is genuine, causing Amelia to reconsider her initial hesitations.

Chapter 8: Internal Conflict/Resistance to Attraction - Richard's POV

As Richard's feelings for Amelia deepen, internal doubts plague him. He grapples with the age gap and fears that his insecurities will sabotage their relationship. Though he is captivated by Amelia's spirit, he questions if he can truly be the kind of partner she deserves. His instincts tell him to push her away to protect her, but the idea of losing her terrifies him.

Chapter 9: Steamy Hot Intimate Scene - Amelia's POV

During a spontaneous night out, Amelia and Richard find themselves getting caught up in a romantic moment that leads to a passionate encounter. They share a night at his luxurious penthouse as they indulge in their attraction. It's a blend of vulnerability, trust, and newfound intimacy. Both are left breathless and transformed, their connection becoming undeniable.

Chapter 10: Internal Falling in Love - Richard's POV

As their relationship continues, Richard acknowledges that he is falling for Amelia. Her laughter, creativity, and kindness infuse his life with joy, revitalizing the parts of him that he thought were lost. However, he struggles with how to integrate her into his world without exposing her to the pressures of his wealthy lifestyle and the high expectations that come with it.

Chapter 11: Dark Moment/Pulling Apart - Amelia's POV

After a public encounter that draws unwanted attention, Amelia overhears a hurtful comment about their age difference and Richard's status. Feeling insecure and pressured by the superficial expectations surrounding them, she confronts Richard. Their emotional confrontation leads to a heated argument, with Richard's fears causing him to unintentionally distance himself from Amelia. Heartbroken, Amelia feels forced to step back, leaving both of them more lost than ever.

Chapter 12: Resolution - Richard's POV

Realizing the gravity of their argument, Richard reflects on the true essence of what he feels for Amelia. He understands that love transcends societal expectations and that he must confront his insecurities head-on. Determined to fight for their relationship, he reaches out to Amelia, expressing his genuine feelings and sharing his desire to build a future together that embraces both their worlds.

Epilogue with HEA - Amelia's POV

Several months later, Amelia and Richard are happily intertwined in their lives. They navigate both the ordinary and the extraordinary together, combining their backgrounds, families, and dreams into a beautiful life. With the support and understanding they've cultivated, they find strength and love in one another, proving that true beauty is found not just in appearances but in the heart. As they share a moment together, gazing into their future, it's clear they've built a love that will last through all of life's seasons.

Billionaire Romance

Outline for Reclusive Billionaire

Chapter 1: Intro to Heroine - Lily's POV

We are introduced to Lily Carter, a compassionate and hardworking nurse in her early thirties. She is dedicated to her job at the local hospital but feels a void in her personal life, often sacrificing her own happiness to care for others. Through her perspective, we glimpse her feelings of loneliness and her dreams of finding true love, which seem to slip further away as she pours herself into her patients.

Chapter 2: Intro to Hero - Kaden's POV

Kaden Sinclair is introduced as a reclusive billionaire, a man defined by his wealth and ruthless business practices. Despite his success, he feels suffocated by his loneliness, and his lack of friendships or meaningful relationships casts a shadow over his life. A flashback reveals Kaden's relentless drive to climb the corporate ladder and the sacrifices he made along the way, which ultimately left him isolated and longing for connection.

Chapter 3: Meet Cute - Lily's POV

After the accident, Lily encounters Kaden for the first time when she begins her shift and is assigned to his care. Initially, she is taken aback by his ruggedly handsome appearance, but the disorientation on his face draws her in. She introduces herself while tending to his injuries, and before long, their brief exchange hints at a deeper connection. Kaden's confusion creates a surreal yet intimate atmosphere, leading to an unexpected spark.

Chapter 4: Growing Attraction/Getting to Know Each Other - Kaden's POV

As days pass, Kaden starts to recover and spends more time with Lily. He appreciates her calm demeanor, intellect, and genuine care as she tends to him. In his slowly returning memory, he finds himself feeling more alive than he has in years, relishing the small joys of their conversations and discovering Lily's passion for her work and life. His growing attraction becomes evident, yet he struggles to accept his feelings due to his uncertain future.

Chapter 5: First Kiss - Lily's POV

One evening, after a long day at work, Lily senses Kaden's frustration with his condition and attempts to lighten the mood. They share laughter and genuine warmth, igniting an undeniable chemistry that culminates in an unexpected and heartwarming first kiss. The moment is electric, filled with vulnerability and hope, but it also leaves Lily in a whirlwind of emotions, questioning the implications of their emerging connection.

Chapter 6: Her Smell - Kaden's POV

As Kaden reflects on his time with Lily during a quiet moment of solitude, he is captivated by the memory of her scent: a mix of lavender and fresh linen that perfectly represents her gentle soul. He realizes he is utterly taken by her beauty, kindness, and the warmth she brings into his life. His friend Lucas, a fellow hospital employee, teases him about his budding affections, making Kaden acutely aware of how far he has fallen for her.

Chapter 7: His Taste - Lily's POV

Alone in her apartment, Lily can't help but replay the kiss in her mind. The taste of Kaden's lips, warm and inviting, lingers on her senses, and she confides in her close friend Mia over a glass of wine. She expresses her confusion about her feelings for a man she hardly knows and her fears of getting hurt, alongside the intense longing she feels for the connection they share.

Chapter 8: Internal Conflict/Resistance to Attraction - Kaden's POV

As Kaden's memory starts returning, he grapples with the return of his old life and the impending reality of his wealth and responsibilities. The contradictions of his feelings for Lily and the life he once led create turmoil within him. He struggles with whether he can offer her anything meaningful when his past looms large over his present, leading him to attempt distancing himself to protect both of them.

Chapter 9: Steamy Hot Intimate Scene - Lily's POV

After an emotionally charged conversation, Lily and Kaden find themselves drawn to each other during a moment of vulnerability. The chemistry ignites into a steamy encounter in the hospital on an off-shift, where they embrace their passion and explore each other intimately. It's a beautiful, heartfelt night that both of them realize may change everything between them.

Chapter 10: Internal Falling in Love - Kaden's POV

Kaden begins to realize that what he feels for Lily is not just attraction; he is falling in love. He thinks about her during moments of solitude, recognizing how she brings light into his world and how her compassion balances out his previously isolated existence. However, the tension between his old life and this newfound love makes him question if he's ready to accept the change.

Chapter 11: Dark Moment/Pulling Apart - Lily's POV

When Kaden's past resurfaces and he regains complete memory of his life before the accident, he exhibits a stark shift. Fearing the impending return to his prior existence, he pushes Lily away, saying he has to focus on his life and responsibilities. Heartbroken, Lily feels abandoned, believing she was merely a temporary escape for Kaden. Their painful separation leaves both grappling with feelings of loss.

Chapter 12: Resolution - Kaden's POV

Determined to embrace the life he truly desires, Kaden realizes that he cannot go back to the isolating world that once defined him. With a newfound sense of purpose, he seeks out Lily, apologizing for his sudden withdrawal. He reveals how much she means to him and how he is ready to build a meaningful relationship, one that includes her and Max, Lily's son, in his life moving forward.

Epilogue with HEA - Lily's POV

Months later, we see Lily and Kaden embracing their new life together—Kaden has embraced his role as not only a partner but a mentor to Max. They navigate life as a blended family, filled with warmth, laughter, and love. The couple reflects on their journey, grateful for the accident that brought them together, as they look forward to a bright future filled with endless possibilities and unconditional love.

Outline for Sweat and Secrets

Chapter 1: Intro to Kerry (Heroine)

- Kerry Adams is introduced as a dedicated fitness coach working with a diverse range of clients. She comes alive in the gym, obsessed with helping others reach their goals.

- We see glimpses of her personal life, where she contemplates her own struggles with balancing her career and personal fulfillment.

Chapter 2: Intro to Clay (Hero)

- Clay Caldwell is painted as the quintessential billionaire, with wealth, prestige, and a secret yearning for genuine connection.

- Flashbacks reveal his past of isolation and gluttony, leading to insecurity about his health and image after years in the limelight.

Chapter 3: Meet Cute

- Kerry receives an unexpected call from Clay's assistant requesting her services. Their awkward first meeting is filled with witty banter, setting the tone for their dynamic.

- Tension arises as Clay tries to mask his vulnerability with bravado, while Kerry sees right through his facade, sparking an interesting connection.

Chapter 4: Growing Attraction/Getting to Know Each Other

- Training sessions begin with awkward moments and intense workouts.

- Through playful challenges and small conversations, Kerry learns about Clay's passions—art, philanthropy, and his secret love for cooking. His charm begins to unravel her guard.

Chapter 5: First Kiss

- After an intense workout, they share a moment of closeness fueled by sweat and adrenaline. A whispered compliment escalates to an unexpected kiss, leaving them both breathless.

- Clay and Kerry are startled, questioning if it was an impulsive mistake or the beginning of something more.

Chapter 6: Her Smell

- Clay can't shake his obsession with Kerry, becoming enamored with the scent of her shampoo and her unique perfume.

- A mutual friend who observes Clay's distraction rib him about his crush, pushing him to confront his feelings. His internal thoughts reveal how he admires her tenacity and warmth.

Chapter 7: His Taste

- Kerry is still reeling from the kiss, confiding in her best friend about how Clay' kiss ignited a spark she'd never expected.

- She reflects on what it means for both their personal and professional relationship. The excitement is mixed with apprehension about crossing lines.

Chapter 8: Internal Conflict/Resistance to Attraction

- Clay struggles with the idea of pursuing a relationship with Kerry, fearing it could jeopardize her career and his reputation.

- Kerry wrestles with her own insecurities, feeling beneath Clay's world of wealth, questioning if she truly fits into his life.

Chapter 9: Steamy Hot Intimate Scene

- Over a candle-lit dinner at Clay's home, the tension culminates into a passionate encounter that deepens their connection.

- They share their vulnerabilities and their fears, breaking down the walls they'd built to protect themselves.

Chapter 10: Internal Falling in Love

- Both characters begin to face their feelings, with Clay realizing he wants Kerry in his life beyond a client.

- Kerry finds herself daydreaming about a future with Clay, but uncertainty looms, as they still struggle with their realities.

Chapter 11: Dark Moment/Pulling Apart

- A scandal involving Clay's company surfaces, putting his world in jeopardy. Kerry fears she will become another burden in his life.

- Misunderstandings and tensions arise, forcing them to confront the reality of their circumstances and their logistics of being together.

Chapter 12: Resolution

- Both characters recalibrate their priorities as Clay fights for his company and confronts what really matters—his health and happiness.

- Kerry realizes her worth and stands by Clay, pushing him to be the best version of himself, leading to reconciliation and stronger bonds.

Epilogue: HEA (Happily Ever After)

- A year later, Clay has rebuilt his company, and Kerry has opened her own fitness studio. They've found a beautiful balance in their personal and professional lives.

- Over a scenic picnic in Central Park, where they reminiscing about their journey, they share a tender promise of a future together, alongside newfound friends and family. Their love story exemplifies that true connections can rejuvenate life, making the everyday remarkable.

Outline for Billionaire's Charm

Chapter 1: Intro to Maya (Heroine)

- Introduce Maya Thompson, a dedicated and hardworking woman who loves nature and values honesty and simplicity. Share her excitement for the vacation she has saved for, juxtaposed with her disdain for materialism, especially in wealth.

- Highlight her past, revealing how her upbringing shaped her beliefs about money and relationships, making her determined to avoid superficial connections.

Chapter 2: Intro to Adrian (Hero)

- Introduce Adrian Kane, the charismatic billionaire known for his opulent lifestyle and the glamorous events he hosts. Show glimpses of his life—parties, business meetings, and the pressures he faces from his family to uphold their legacy.

- Reveal Adrian's hidden struggles with the expectations of wealth and how he often yearns for authenticity amid the superficiality that surrounds him.

Chapter 3: Meet Cute

- Set the scene as Maya arrives on the island and quickly becomes aware of its luxurious charm, feeling out of place. At the beach, a sudden storm hits, forcing her to seek shelter.

- While running for cover, she collides with Adrian, who is trying to secure his yacht. Their first meeting is filled with tension and banter, as Maya expresses her irritation at his carefree, materialistic attitude while Adrian is amused by her fiery spirit.

Chapter 4: Growing Attraction/Getting to Know Each Other

- Stranded together in the aftermath of the storm, Maya and Adrian find themselves working side by side to help those affected on the island. As they share stories and vulnerabilities, they uncover common interests and slowly start to bond.

- Moments of laughter and playful teasing jar their initial impressions of one another, leading to unexpected flirtation that both resist.

Chapter 5: First Kiss

- After a day filled with hard work restoring the island, Maya stumbles upon Adrian's secret garden. The ambiance is peaceful, creating a moment of intimacy. They share a heartfelt conversation about childhood dreams and the pressures of their lives.

- Their emotional connection mounts, and they share their first kiss—a soft yet electric moment that catches them both off guard, awakening feelings neither expected.

Chapter 6: Her Smell

- Following the kiss, Adrian can't shake the memory of Maya's refreshing scent—the blend of ocean breeze and a hint of coconut oil. He becomes increasingly drawn to her.

- A friend or colleague whom Adrian confides in during a call notices his distracted demeanor and teases him, making Adrian work harder to hide the attraction blooming inside him.

Chapter 7: His Taste

- Alone in her cabin, Maya reflectively recalls the kiss, replaying each moment in her mind. She confides in her best friend over the phone, excited yet fearful about where their connection could lead. The taste of Adrian lingers in her thoughts—complex, thrilling, and unlike anything she's ever experienced.

- This moment emboldens Maya, revealing how her heart longs for the adventure of love but fears the notion of getting hurt by someone like Adrian.

Chapter 8: Internal Conflict/Resistance to Attraction

- Adrian grapples with his growing feelings for Maya, conflicting with his perception as a man of wealth and the lifestyle he represents. Memories of past romantic endeavors, which were often transactional or shallow, haunt him.

- Maya, on the other hand, battles her disdain for Adrian's materialistic world. She starts seeing glimpses of his vulnerability but struggles to balance her desire and severe apprehension toward a relationship that could bring heartache.

Chapter 9: Steamy Hot Intimate Scene

- One evening, the tension reaches a boiling point as a romantic dinner is set up on the beach. Under the stars, they indulge in laughter, sharing heartfelt stories around a table adorned with candles and flowers.

- The moment transitions into passionate intimacy as they explore each other in the privacy of Adrian's villa—vulnerability mingling with desire, where walls come down, and they let go of their fears, succumbing to their feelings.

Chapter 10: Internal Falling in Love

- Despite their steamy encounter, both Maya and Adrian are left pondering the implications of their relationship. With every interaction, Maya discovers how genuine and thoughtful Adrian is—not just the glamourous image the world sees.

- Adrian falls deeper for Maya, recognizing her impact on him. Her passion for life and nature helps him see the world in a more profound way.

Chapter 11: Dark Moment/Pulling Apart

- Just as everything seems to align, news arrives that the storm has caused significant damage to both the island and Adrian's family business, creating chaos. Adrian's family demands his immediate return, pulling him away from Maya.

- Miscommunication leads Maya to believe Adrian is simply a wealthy playboy who will return to his old life, and she begins to doubt their connection. Hurt, she feels abandoned, and their emotional distance grows, leaving both hearts heavy.

Chapter 12: Resolution

- Realizing that he cannot live without Maya, Adrian confronts his family and decides to take control of his future rather than remain a pawn to the family empire. He returns to the island, finding Maya in a secluded spot, dancing alone in the wind.

- In a heartfelt exchange, they confront their fears, expressing their love and commitment to one another despite the obstacles ahead. They come to terms with their differences and find common ground.

Epilogue: HEA (Happily Ever After)

- Months later, Maya has taken a role in the island's restoration efforts and has found a renewed purpose in her life. Adrian has successfully modernized his family business, advocating for sustainable practices that benefit both the community and the environment.

- They are depicted as partners in every sense, planning their future together while seamlessly blending their worlds. In the island's warm glow, they share a dance on the beach—reminding us that love, like nature, can thrive even after the fiercest storms.

Outline for Fortune's Embrace

Chapter 1: Intro to Evelyn (Heroine)

- Introduce Evelyn Carter, a driven and intelligent woman entrenched in her family's legacy of success. Reveal her ambition as she navigates the corporate world, trying to prove herself beyond her family name.

- Explore her inner conflict about following her family's path versus her desire to forge her own identity. Showcase snippets of her life, including family dinners filled with discussions about legal affairs that steer her toward unease about their methods.

Chapter 2: Intro to Nathaniel (Hero)

- Introduce Nathaniel Hayes, a billionaire businessman whose relentless ambition has driven him to the heights of entrepreneurial success. Illustrate his charismatic persona, while hinting at the toll his recent legal battle with Evelyn's family has taken on him.

- Present moments of vulnerability that reveal Nathaniel's weariness from the courtroom drama, leaving him feeling defeated despite his wealth—an internal battle between pride and the desire to rebuild.

Chapter 3: Meet Cute

- Describe the awkward yet passionate first encounter between Evelyn and Nathaniel at a charity event related to the legal battle. They engage in a heated but covert argument when Evelyn accidentally spills her drink on him.

- Their encounter is full of tension, both fueled by their past and initial hatred. The chemistry is palpable, leading to a mix of irritation and unexpected intrigue.

Chapter 4: Growing Attraction/Getting to Know Each Other

- As they are forced to collaborate on the rebuilding project for Nathaniel's brand, their interactions become increasingly charged. Evelyn starts to see Nathaniel beyond the mogul image—his charisma and creativity shine as they brainstorm ideas.

- They begin to share personal experiences and fears, slowly peeking beyond the walls built by their families. Both feel an undeniable attraction that is both thrilling and unsettling.

Chapter 5: First Kiss

- During an intense and late-night brainstorming session, the tension reaches a crescendo, leading to a moment where they are caught up in each other's company. Overwhelmed by emotions, they share their first electrifying kiss, illuminated by the dying embers of a fire they had lit to fuel their creativity.

- Both of them are startled by the intensity and rush of feelings the kiss evokes—something they cannot ignore.

Chapter 6: Her Smell

- Nathaniel reflects on the kiss, haunted by the lingering scent of Evelyn's floral perfume mixed with the faintest hint of lavender. It reminds him of her warmth and vulnerability.

- A friend, a humor-driven co-worker, notices Nathaniel's distracted demeanor and playfully teases him about Evelyn, prompting him to confront his growing feelings for her.

Chapter 7: His Taste

- Alone in her apartment, Evelyn can't help but replay the kiss in her head, allowing herself a moment of fantasy about Nathaniel. She confides in her sister, expressing both excitement and confusion about the attraction that has developed, saying he tasted like ambition and compassion.

- Her sister encourages her to explore these feelings but warns her about the potential fallout with their families.

Chapter 8: Internal Conflict/Resistance to Attraction

- Nathaniel struggles with the implications of his growing feelings for Evelyn. He is torn between wanting to embrace this unexpected relationship and fearing the fallout from their families' rivalry.

- Evelyn, too, is trapped in turmoil, feeling betrayal toward her family for even considering a relationship with the man they fought against. Guilt and longing battle within her.

Chapter 9: Steamy Hot Intimate Scene

- In a moment of vulnerability following a significant breakthrough in their project, Nathaniel invites Evelyn to his luxurious condo to celebrate their achievements. With the thrill of success and wine flowing, they end up in a heated moment that leads to passion.

- They share a steamy and intimate encounter, losing themselves in each other. This physical connection strengthens their bond but leaves them questioning their moral standings.

Chapter 10: Internal Falling in Love

- Following their intimate night, both Nathaniel and Evelyn wake up glowing yet fraught with confusion. Through their work, Nathaniel learns to trust in a new vision for his life thanks to Evelyn's influence, while she discovers her own strength through his support.

- They begin to realize that love is blossoming between them, regardless of the complications that surround their respective families.

Chapter 11: Dark Moment/Pulling Apart

- Tensions escalate as Evelyn's family discovers her relationship with Nathaniel. They confront her, warning her about associating with the enemy and pressuring her to sever all ties. Heartbroken, Evelyn feels forced to choose her family's allegiance over her personal happiness.

- Nathaniel, feeling abandoned and betrayed, pulls away, believing she prioritizes her family's demands over their newfound love. Both are left in pain, their worlds apart once again.

Chapter 12: Resolution

- After a few days of separation, Evelyn reflects on her true desires and comes to terms with her feelings for Nathaniel. She realizes that she cannot let her family's choices dictate her life. In a bold move, she reaches out to Nathaniel, expressing her determination to reclaim her happiness.

- They reunite, declaring their love despite the obstacles. Together, they devise a plan to address their family's rivalry, vowing to rebuild not only Nathaniel's fortune but a united front together.

Epilogue: HEA (Happily Ever After)

- Several months later, Nathaniel and Evelyn have made significant progress, launching a groundbreaking company that blends both of their visions. They host a joint charity event, symbolizing unity and the possibilities forged from love.

- Surrounded by friends and family, they steal a kiss under a twinkling sky, showcasing not just the wealth of love but the beauty of their journey together—a reminder that true fortune comes from the heart.

Outline for Crowned Hearts

Chapter 1: Intro to Isabella (Heroine)

- Introduce Isabella "Izzy" Thompson, a hardworking scholarship student at a prestigious British university. Explore her struggles, aspirations, and the pressure of fitting into a world filled with privilege.

- Highlight her background, family dynamics, and her passion for her studies, showcasing her independence and determination to succeed despite financial constraints.

Chapter 2: Intro to Alexander (Hero)

- Present Prince Alexander of Wales as the charming and charismatic heir to the throne, revealing his dual life—publicly regal yet privately yearning for normalcy.

- Delve into his responsibilities, the weight of expectations from his family, and his struggles with the media's invasive gaze. Demonstrate his desire to find authentic connections beyond his royal persona.

Chapter 3: Meet Cute

- Describe the serendipitous meeting at the university pub, where Izzy and Alex lock eyes amidst the busy crowd. Their conversation flows effortlessly as they bond over shared interests, unaware of each other's true identities.

- The chemistry between them is electric, leading to laughter and flirtation that feels like an escape from their respective lives.

Chapter 4: Growing Attraction/Getting to Know Each Other

- Explore their growing rapport through casual dates and encounters on campus, diving deeper into their personalities, dreams, and vulnerabilities.

- They share secrets and stories, discovering the exquisite joy of being with someone who sees them for who they are, free from titles or judgments.

Chapter 5: First Kiss

- During a quiet moment at a picturesque spot on campus—perhaps during a sunset—their connection culminates in a passionate first kiss that ignites feelings they both attempted to resist.

- The kiss is tender yet electric, leaving both of them breathless and confused about the implications of their romance.

Chapter 6: Her Smell

- Alex reflects on the kiss and the lingering scent of Izzy's floral perfume that still clings to him, reminding him of her warmth and openness.

- As he walks through the university grounds, a close friend, noticing his distracted demeanor and the way he lights up when he mentions Izzy, teases him about being smitten, prompting Alex to confront his feelings head-on.

Chapter 7: His Taste

- Back in her apartment, Izzy revels in stolen moments and relives the kiss, recalling how Alexander's lips tasted and her feelings of exhilaration mixed with confusion.

- She confides in her best friend about her feelings for Alex, grappling with the excitement of their romance and the fears surfacing regarding his true identity.

Chapter 8: Internal Conflict/Resistance to Attraction

- Alex faces uncertainty as the pressures of royal responsibilities loom larger, leaving him questioning whether he can pursue something real with Izzy while maintaining his obligations to the crown.

- Izzy wrestles with her own doubts, feeling unworthy of being with a prince, battling her insecurities about whether she can truly fit into his world.

Chapter 9: Steamy Hot Intimate Scene

- After a very successful night out at a charity gala that Izzy attends as Alexander's "date," they return to his private estate for an intimate celebration of their connection. The atmosphere is charged, and they share a passionate night together.

- The scene highlights their physical attraction, emotional vulnerability, and mutual longing. They find solace in one another, allowing themselves to escape the outside pressures for a night.

Chapter 10: Internal Falling in Love

- As time passes, both Alex and Izzy realize they are falling deeply in love, embracing the beauty of their unexpected relationship. They simply enjoy each other's company—studying late into the night, attending art exhibits, and sharing moments that reveal their true selves.

- Alex begins to envision a future beyond royal duty, while Izzy feels supported and cherished in a way she never thought possible.

Chapter 11: Dark Moment/Pulling Apart

- News of their relationship breaks, creating a media frenzy and public scrutiny that puts pressure on both their lives. Izzy faces harsh judgment and scrutiny, being labeled a "gold digger."

- Simultaneously, Alex is pressured by his family to end the relationship for the sake of royal tradition and duty. Faced with the anguish of potential scandal, he pushes Izzy away, believing it's for her protection. Their love is suddenly overshadowed by heartache and confusion.

Chapter 12: Resolution

- After a period of separation filled with soul-searching, Izzy learns to believe in her worth and her right to love freely. Meanwhile, Alex confronts his family about his feelings for her, challenging the status quo.

- Their paths converge again as they come to realize that love cannot be dictated by royal expectations or social standings. They find a way to communicate openly, unlocking the strength they built together.

Epilogue: HEA (Happily Ever After)

- Set a year later at a royal garden party, Alex introduces Izzy with pride. She has become a beloved figure, breaking social barriers, and launching charitable initiatives tied to her own passions.

- Together, they dance under the stars, their relationship a testament to love conquering all obstacles. Their future is bright with shared dreams, and they stand united, ready to face whatever comes their way.

Outline for Caught in the Crossfire of Love~Billionaire Mafia
Chapter 1: Intro to Heroine (Luna's POV)

Luna Hayes, an optimistic and kind-hearted recent college graduate, introduces herself while recounting her passion for life and her dream of love. Working at a local café in Montclair, she feels the thrill of new possibilities and a fresh start. Despite her naivety, her heart yearns for a significant connection that will redefine her life.

Chapter 2: Intro to Hero (Alex's POV)

Alex Russo is portrayed as the charming, confident heir to a notorious mob family. Amidst the glitz of nightlife and unspoken threats, he grapples with the weight of his legacy. Despite the adrenaline that his lifestyle brings him, Alex longs for authenticity and connection but fears being tied down—until he meets someone who could change everything.

Chapter 3: Meet Cute (Luna's POV)

One sunny afternoon, Luna takes her golden retriever, Bella, to the local dog park. As Bella runs wild, chasing after a ball, she accidentally collides with Alex, who is training his impressive German Shepherd. The two dogs instantly hit it off, while Luna and Alex engage in a lighthearted conversation about their furry companions. As they try to corral the dogs and prevent them from creating chaos, Luna can't help but notice Alex's easygoing nature and the depth in his eyes. Their playful back-and-forth leads to Luna sharing her favorite dog training tips, and Alex invites her to join them for a follow-up doggy playdate, enamored by her spirit and warmth.

Chapter 4: Growing Attraction/Getting to Know Each Other (Alex's POV)

As Luna frequently visits the café, Alex finds himself drawn to her sweetness and sincerity. They start spending time together, sharing stories and dreams—Luna blissfully unaware of the intricacies of Alex's life. He feels a profound pull toward her but remains wary of opening up about his true self, as secrets loom in the shadows.

Chapter 5: First Kiss (Luna's POV)

On a romantic evening stroll, Luna and Alex stop beside a fountain, a moment where their eyes lock, and the world melts away. The tension builds as they share their first kiss—the spark igniting a fire within

Luna. She feels alive and exhilarated, caught in a whirlwind romance that is more than she ever imagined.

Chapter 6: Her Smell (Alex's POV)

During a quiet moment reflecting on Luna, Alex is consumed by her intoxicating scent—a mix of vanilla and summer blooms that lingers with him. Confiding in his best friend Marco, he admits how deeply he is falling for her. Marco teases him about being whipped, but Alex brushes it off, acknowledging that Luna brings light to his otherwise dark life.

Chapter 7: His Taste (Luna's POV)

While confiding in her best friend Clara, Luna describes her feelings for Alex and how intoxicating their kiss was. She can't seem to shake her thoughts about their chemistry, even wondering how she got so lucky. However, there's a slight twinge of unease when she recounts the intensity of Alex's gaze, but she brushes it off, focusing instead on the excitement of new love.

Chapter 8: Internal Conflict/Resistance to Attraction (Alex's POV)

Alex begins to struggle with his dual life. Torn between his love for Luna and the loyalty to his family's legacy, he attempts to distance himself from her, fearing that his world will pull her into danger. He battles with the desire to be with her while wrestling with the darker aspects of his reality—her innocence at risk in his chaotic life.

Chapter 9: Steamy Hot Intimate Scene (Luna's POV)

While attending a friend's party where Alex is present, emotions run high. In a moment of passionate connection fueled by love and longing, Luna and Alex take their relationship to the next level. The night is filled with heated exchanges as they explore their desires, unaware of the impending storm surrounding them.

Chapter 10: Internal Falling in Love (Alex's POV)

As their relationship deepens, Alex is confronted with unexpected feelings of love for Luna. He admires her unwavering belief in the good, her lighthearted laughter, and the way she sees warmth in everyone. While he grapples with fear of exposing her to his family's business, he cannot deny the growing bond that connects them.

Chapter 11: Dark Moment/Pulling Apart (Luna's POV)

Luna accidentally stumbles upon a secret meeting between Alex and his family, mistaking it for a close-knit gathering. The unease grows when she overhears plans that hint at the darker side of Alex's world. Confronting him leads to a heartbreaking realization that Alex has been keeping significant secrets—the truth shattering the trust she had in him.

Chapter 12: Resolution (Alex's POV)

Alex, struggling with guilt and regret, realizes he cannot fight his feelings for Luna or his desire to keep her safe. Determined to prove his love, he confronts his family, seeking a way to distance himself from the life they lead. He makes clear his intentions to protect Luna, promising to make changes for their future, even if it risks drawing the family's ire.

Epilogue with HEA (Luna's POV)

Months later, Luna reflects on how she has transformed, stepping into her power while maintaining her compassionate heart. She and Alex navigate their love while cautiously intertwining their lives. In a heartfelt moment, Alex surprises her at the café with a proposal, affirming his commitment to her and promising a life built on love rather than secrets. As their future shines brightly, they stand surrounded by family and friends, ready to embrace whatever comes next, side by side.

Title: Bids for the Heart

Chapter 1: Intro to Heroine (Dani's POV)

Meet Danielle Greene, a vibrant yet recently heartbroken artist who is dedicated to her craft but struggles with the aftermath of her last relationship. We delve into her world as she prepares for the charity auction, emphasizing her passion for artistic expression and a sense of obligation to support local causes. Despite her spirited nature, an air of vulnerability surrounds her as she navigates through her plans for the future.

Chapter 2: Intro to Hero (Mac's POV)

Introduce Mackenzie Harrington, the charismatic and sophisticate local businessman with a passion for philanthropy. We explore his motivation for supporting the charity auction, revealing his commitment to bettering the community and an underlying sense of loneliness amidst his success. Mac's childhood shaped him into a compassionate yet guarded man, making him wary of letting people in.

Chapter 3: Meet Cute (Dani's POV)

Dani has a comedic mishap at the charity auction where she accidentally bids on a date with Mac, barely knowing him. The tension and awkwardness of the moment set a playful tone as Dani grapples with the unexpected burden of winning the date. Mac finds her charming and spirited, offering an opportunity for light-hearted banter, despite her embarrassment.

Chapter 4: Growing Attraction/Getting to Know Each Other (Mac's POV)

Mac reflects on the bid, now seeing Dani in a new light. Their first date, filled with unexpected laughter and genuine conversation, allows Mac to reveal his passion for philanthropy. He finds himself captivated by Dani's creativity and her infectious energy. Their bond deepens as they attend planning sessions for the charity, fostering emotional connection.

Chapter 5: First Kiss (Dani's POV)

During a picturesque sunset picnic arranged for the charity, Dani feels a magnetic pull towards Mac. As they share a warm moment and laughter, an unexpected kiss unfolds. Dani feels a whirlwind of emotions as sparks fly, leaving her breathless and confused about her feelings for Mac and what it might mean for their fake relationship.

Chapter 6: His Smell (Mac's POV)

While reflecting at home after their picnic, Mac savors the lingering scent of Dani: a blend of floral perfume and her natural warmth. His thoughts drift to her beauty, captivating smile, and the way her eyes light up when she talks about her art. Mac confides in his best friend about how his feelings for Dani are becoming more real and meaningful.

Chapter 7: Her Taste (Dani's POV)

Later that night, Dani can't shake off the feeling of their kiss. Alone in her studio, she recalls the way Mac's lips felt, how his unexpected sweetness mixed with the taste of the wine they shared. In a conversation with her sister, she admits how the kiss ignited something inside her that she's not ready to confront, fearing the complexity it may bring to their budding relationship.

Chapter 8: Internal Conflict/Resistance to Attraction (Mac's POV)

Despite their growing connection, Mac's fears begin to emerge. He battles with the idea of falling for Dani versus his desire to keep things simple and uncomplicated. Reminded of past heartbreaks, he confides in his sister, who challenges him to embrace vulnerability instead of running. Ultimately, he realizes that his connection with Dani feels too valuable to let go.

Chapter 9: Steamy Hot Intimate Scene (Dani's POV)

After a charity event where emotions run high, tension erupts into passion. Dani and Mac share a heated moment filled with longing that escalates to a passionate embrace. The intimacy transforms their relationship, leaving Dani exhilarated yet conflicted about how to navigate the resulting shift from a fake romance to authentic connection.

Chapter 10: Internal Falling in Love (Mac's POV)

Mac grapples with the reality that he's genuinely falling for Dani as he thinks about her brightening his days. He recalls shared memories and how she has made him feel alive again, leading him to realize love is worth the risk. The bond they share is utterly unique, stirring both excitement and fear as he contemplates a future together.

Chapter 11: Dark Moment/Pulling Apart (Dani's POV)

Dani discovers Mac's initial intent to treat their relationship as a mere bet for charity. Feeling hurt and abandoned, she pulls away, thinking he never intended to care for her. She confronts him, leading to a passionate argument, which ends in heartache and uncertainty about their future. The emotional fallout leaves both of them reeling.

Chapter 12: Resolution (Mac's POV)

Mac realizes he cannot let Dani slip away without fighting for their love. He seeks her out, pouring out his true feelings in a heartfelt apology, revealing just how much he's come to care for her beyond the pretense. Their candid conversation brings clarity and understanding, reigniting the love that blossomed between them.

Epilogue: Happily Ever After (HEA) (Both POVs)

Months later, Dani and Mac are thriving as a couple, combining their passions for art and philanthropy. Attending a new charity event, their playful banter refills the air, and they reminisce about the wild events that brought them together. They share a tender moment, solidifying their commitment and celebrating a love that transformed from a playful wager into a heartfelt partnership, promising a bright future filled with joy and purpose.

Outline for The Billionaire's Bet

Chapter 1: Intro to Heroine (Amelia's POV)

Amelia Harper is introduced as a fiercely independent businesswoman, driven and ambitious, juggling multiple projects to make a name for herself in the competitive world of event planning. Her passion for charity work is a driving force in her life, and she dreams of a better future while struggling to pay off student debts.

Chapter 2: Intro to Hero (Alex's POV)

We meet Alex Sterling, a dashing billionaire known for his philanthropic efforts but also for his public persona as a shrewd businessman. Despite his wealth, he feels trapped by societal expectations and the family legacy he's built—a façade that hides his vulnerabilities and past heartaches.

Chapter 3: Meet Cute (Amelia's POV)

At the charity auction, Amelia confronts Alex, who is charmingly arrogant while placing his bids. They lock eyes over the auction podium when she realizes he's just won the vacation she desperately wanted. Their heated exchange carries an unexpected spark of chemistry, setting the stage for rivalry.

Chapter 4: Growing Attraction/Getting to Know Each Other (Alex's POV)

While planning their competitive excursions related to the wager, Alex begins to shed light on his life. He grows intrigued by Amelia's fire and ambition. Bonding through shared interests in charity work, their playful interactions lead to a growing attraction he can't ignore.

Chapter 5: First Kiss (Amelia's POV)

After an evening at a charity gala where they are forced to act as a couple for the media, tensions rise. A miscommunication leads to a passionate kiss in a secluded garden, leaving Amelia breathless and questioning her feelings for this man who seems so different from her initial impression.

Chapter 6: Her Smell (Alex's POV)

After their kiss, Alex finds himself unable to focus. Memories of Amelia's intoxicating perfume and the warmth of her body linger, pulling him into reflections about her beauty and the way her smile lights up a room. Confiding in his best friend, he admits he may be falling for her, terrified of breaking his own rules.

Chapter 7: His Taste (Amelia's POV)

In the aftermath of their kiss, Amelia can't shake the feeling of Alex's lips on hers. When she confides in her best friend during a coffee date, she expresses confusion about her blossoming feelings for him and the reality that he represents a world far from her own.

Chapter 8: Internal Conflict/Resistance to Attraction (Alex's POV)

As their connection deepens, Alex grapples with his attraction to Amelia, fearing that her dreams and ambitions might clash violently with his own hidden fears. The disparity between their worlds hammers at his conscience, and he wrestles with the idea of letting her in, terrified of losing control.

Chapter 9: Steamy Hot Intimate Scene (Amelia's POV)

During a weekend trip as part of the wager, the chemistry reaches a boiling point. Alone in a luxurious suite, they give in to their desires, sharing an intoxicating night filled with passion that reveals their vulnerabilities and deepens their bond.

Chapter 10: Internal Falling in Love (Alex's POV)

Post-encounter, Alex realizes he has fallen for Amelia, recognizing that what he once resisted is now an undeniable truth. He confides in his sister about how she makes him feel—like he can be unapologetically himself—and how that scares him just as much as it excites him.

Chapter 11: Dark Moment/Pulling Apart (Amelia's POV)

After overhearing a conversation about Alex's supposed engagement to another woman promoting a luxury brand, Amelia's insecurities surface. Feeling betrayed, she pulls away and confronts him, leading to a hurtful argument where they both voice unspoken fears and misunderstandings about their relationship.

Chapter 12: Resolution (Alex's POV)

In the wake of their fight and the painful distance that follows, Alex realizes he cannot let Amelia go without a fight. After heartfelt reflection, he decides to publicly declare his feelings and confront the rumors about an engagement, seeking a clear path towards a future with her.

Epilogue: With HEA (Amelia's POV)

Several months later, Amelia and Alex have found their footing together, balancing their lives between charity work and romance. Alex stands at the podium during a major charity event, proclaiming his love for Amelia, who stands beaming in the crowd. Their journey has led them to a shared life, filled with promise and adventure, sealing their happily ever after.

Outline for Love in High Places

Chapter 1: Intro to Heroine (Leanne's POV)

Leanne Howell is introduced as a fiercely independent journalist with a reputation for uncovering the truth. Working for a prominent publication, she's ambitious and determined to make her mark in a male-dominated field. Her skepticism towards the wealthy stems from her own background, and she's known for her no-holds-barred interview style.

Chapter 2: Intro to Hero (Holden's POV)

Holden Devereaux, a billionaire philanthropist, is introduced as a charismatic figure who has risen to prominence through his charitable endeavors. Behind his charm lies a complex past filled with personal loss and burdens that have shaped his desire to give back to society. His public persona is that of an altruist, but few know the man grappling with shadows of his history.

Chapter 3: Meet Cute (Leanne's POV)

Leanne meets Holden in a crowded press conference announcing his latest philanthropic initiative. Their encounter is charged with tension—Holden makes a bold statement about his commitment to transparency, and Leanne challenges him on the potential hypocrisy of billionaires. Sparks fly, and the friction between them becomes palpable as she refuses to back down in her questioning.

Chapter 4: Growing Attraction/Getting to Know Each Other (Holden's POV)

As Leanne prepares for their exclusive interview, Holden finds himself intrigued by her intelligence and determination. During the interview, he opens up about his motivations and dreams, recognizing an unexpected connection forming between them. Leanne's sharp wit and insight captivate him, and he yearns to know more about the woman behind the journalist façade.

Chapter 5: First Kiss (Leanne's POV)

After a revealing interview at an art gala that showcases one of Holden's charitable projects, Leanne and Holden find themselves alone on a terrace overlooking the city. The atmosphere is electric, and amidst the sea of lights, they share a passionate kiss that takes them both by surprise, leaving Leanne breathless as she confronts her feelings for him.

Chapter 6: Her Smell (Holden's POV)

Following the kiss, Holden can't focus on his charitable commitments. Memories of Leanne flood his mind. Her captivating fragrance—a mix of fresh flowers and a hint of citrus—lingers with him, making him nostalgic for that moment on the terrace. Alone in his office, he confides in his best friend, expressing how Leanne has shattered the walls he built around his heart.

Chapter 7: His Taste (Leanne's POV)

Back at her apartment, Leanne relives the kiss and how Holden's lips ignited something within her. Confiding in her roommate, she admits to feeling a whirlwind of emotions—confusion about her attraction and fear that his wealth might ultimately separate them. The kiss plays over and over in her mind, highlighting her internal struggle.

Chapter 8: Internal Conflict/Resistance to Attraction (Holden's POV)

As Holden becomes more aware of his feelings, he battles his insecurities about their differing social statuses. He worries Leanne might only be interested in him for his fame or wealth. He recalls the expectations placed on him by family and society, prompting him to question whether he can truly let her into his world, knowing the potential backlash.

Chapter 9: Steamy Hot Intimate Scene (Leanne's POV)

During a rare evening together at Holden's luxurious penthouse, the tension between them builds until they give in to their desires. The night is filled with passion, exploration, and an overwhelming sense of connection that leaves both of them craving more than just a physical relationship. It marks a turning point in their bond.

Chapter 10: Internal Falling in Love (Holden's POV)

In the days that follow, Holden is consumed by thoughts of Leanne. He starts to embrace the idea of being with her, enjoying her tenacity, humor, and warmth. He has moments of introspection, realizing he enjoys her company and finds solace in their shared conversations. He begins to consider a future that includes her, despite their complicated circumstances.

Chapter 11: Dark Moment/Pulling Apart (Leanne's POV)

Misunderstandings arise when Leanne discovers a rumor about Holden's alleged engagement to a socialite to further his public image. Feeling heartbroken and betrayed, she confronts him, leading to a heated argument that forces them to confront their inner demons and the realities of life in the limelight. Leanne retreats, convinced that their worlds are too different.

Chapter 12: Resolution (Holden's POV)

Devastated by the fallout, Holden realizes he cannot let Leanne walk away. He reaches out, determined to clarify the misunderstandings and profess his love. During a public charity event, he bravely declares his affections for Leanne, dispelling rumors and proving that his feelings for her are genuine. Confronting the truths about their relationship, they mend their bond, ready to face the challenges ahead.

Epilogue: With HEA (Leanne's POV)

Several months later, Leanne and Holden are navigating their relationship together with newfound trust. Having collaborated on a charity project, they are public advocates for change—not just as a couple but as partners who uplift each other. In a quieter moment at a café, Leanne realizes that love can thrive in high places, and she watches Holden from across the table, feeling grateful for the journey they've embarked upon together—a journey filled with hope, love, and endless possibility.

Outline for The Runaway Heiress

Chapter 1: Intro to Heroine (Amelia's POV)

Amelia Sinclair feels trapped in her life of opulence as her engagement party approaches. She reflects on her privileged upbringing, her family's expectations, and the persona she's supposed to maintain. As she escapes her lavish apartment, she glimpses at the life she truly desires—one filled with authenticity and love.

Chapter 2: Intro to Hero (Jack's POV)

Jack Rivers stands on the rugged cliffs of Red Harbor, staring out at the ocean and contemplating his life as a struggling artist. Haunted by personal loss and the shadows of his upbringing, he has built an emotional wall around himself, determined not to let anyone in. He finds solace in painting but struggles with feelings of isolation.

Chapter 3: Meet Cute (Amelia's POV)

While exploring the quaint town of Red Harbor, Amelia accidentally ducks into a local café to escape a sudden downpour. Drenched, she bumps into Jack and he catches her before she falls. They share an awkward but charming exchange, igniting an unexpected spark. Amelia feels a rush of thrill and fear at meeting someone so different from her world.

Chapter 4: Growing Attraction/Getting to Know Each Other (Jack's POV)

As Amelia becomes a regular at the café, Jack finds himself drawn to her vibrant energy and genuine curiosity. Amid painting and café banter, they begin to share stories, and Jack finds a surprising connection with her. He admires her determination to live in the moment, feeling a mix of admiration and confusion about his growing interest.

Chapter 5: First Kiss (Amelia's POV)

During a day spent exploring the stunning coastline, Amelia and Jack share laughter and stories that flow seamlessly between them. Under the backdrop of a breathtaking sunset, their chemistry culminates in an electrifying kiss, filled with passion and the promise of something deeper. Amelia is overwhelmed by her emotions, both elation and fear of what lies ahead.

Chapter 6: Her Smell (Jack's POV)

After their kiss, Jack can't shake the scent of Amelia—the ocean breeze mingled with a hint of her floral perfume. Alone in his studio, he recalls her beauty and playful smile. He confides in his best friend, struggling to articulate his feelings and the intensity of his attraction. Jack begins to realize how pivotal Amelia has become in his life.

Chapter 7: His Taste (Amelia's POV)

Alone in her rented cottage, Amelia reflects on the kiss, replaying every moment in her mind. She confides in her old friend via video call, sharing how Jack's kiss felt electric, awakening emotions she thought were long buried. Amelia grapples with the reality and thrill of falling for someone who lives a world so far removed from her own.

Chapter 8: Internal Conflict/Resistance to Attraction (Jack's POV)

Despite the undeniable chemistry, Jack wrestles with his emotional scars and hesitates to let Amelia into his heart. Fear of being hurt again clashes with his growing attraction. He feels unworthy of her affections, leading him to create emotional distance, pushing her away just as their bond strengthens.

Chapter 9: Steamy Hot Intimate Scene (Amelia's POV)

Circumstances lead to an intimate night spent together at Jack's studio. Wrapped in the heat of the moment, they share a raw and passionate night that deepens their connection. Although overwhelmed by the intensity of their feelings, Amelia feels as if she is finally unraveling the closure and fears that have followed her.

Chapter 10: Internal Falling in Love (Jack's POV)

In the weeks that follow, Jack cannot ignore that he is falling deeply in love with Amelia. He begins to envision a future with her—until he's confronted by memories of his past. He finds himself questioning if he can truly embrace this new relationship and become the man Amelia deserves. Jack grapples with the idea of vulnerability.

Chapter 11: Dark Moment/Pulling Apart (Amelia's POV)

When Amelia's family arrives in Red Harbor to bring her back to her former life, she faces mounting pressure. She realizes that Jack is now in the crosshairs of her old world, leading to a heartbreaking confrontation. After an emotional fight, she leaves Jack, feeling trapped between two worlds and wrecked by the fear of losing him.

Chapter 12: Resolution (Jack's POV)

After a period of reflection and soul-searching, Jack decides he cannot lose Amelia. Fueled by determination, he confronts his fears and realizes he deserves to fight for the love they share. He devises a plan to show her the life they could build together, confident in their connection despite the challenges.

Epilogue: HEA (Amelia's POV)

Months later, Amelia stands on the cliffs of Red Harbor, feeling the salty breeze on her face. She watches as Jack paints beside her.

They've created a life together, merging their worlds and dreams. With a newfound sense of purpose, Amelia is no longer the runaway heiress; she is a woman empowered by love, ready to embrace a future alongside Jack, fulfilling both their desires for authenticity and passion.

Holiday Romance

Title: Wrapped in Love

Chapter 1: Sienna's POV - Intro to Heroine

Sienna Reynolds is introduced as a spirited young woman in her late twenties who juggles a demanding job as a marketing specialist and her creative side hustles, which include baking festive treats. Though she contributes daily to social media marketing, she often feels disconnected from genuine relationships and romantic possibilities, caught in a routine. With Christmas approaching, Sienna longs for magic in her life and hopes to rekindle her passion for seasonal festivities.

Chapter 2: Noah's POV - Intro to Hero

Noah Blake is introduced as a charming thirty-something entrepreneur who has just launched his holiday basket company, Festive Faves. Known for his work ethic and determination, he has poured his heart into the business after a challenging year. However, despite his professional success, he struggles with loneliness and the fear of truly opening up to someone, harboring doubts about the authenticity of modern romance amidst technology.

Chapter 3: Meet Cute (Sienna's POV)

Sienna stumbles upon the Instagram ad for Festive Faves while mindlessly scrolling one evening. After impulsively double-tapping the post, she is surprised to find a personal message from Noah the next day, introducing himself and the company. Though a bit flustered, she responds, seeing this as a chance to break her routine and engage in a playful banter, unaware of how significant this interaction will become.

Chapter 4: Growing Attraction/Getting to Know Each Other (Noah's POV)

Noah is both excited and bewildered by Sienna's engaging energy and humor in their messages. Their conversations evolve quickly, as they share their holiday traditions, and Noah feels his walls start to lower. He finds himself thinking about Sienna constantly and cherishes their exchanges more than he originally anticipated. He admires her creativity and zest for life, feeling drawn to her authenticity.

Chapter 5: First Kiss (Sienna's POV)

On Christmas Eve, they finally meet at the festive market that Noah invited Sienna to. After spending the evening enjoying the ambiance, sharing laughs, and attempting to concoct their holiday baskets, the moment culminates in a gentle yet electrifying first kiss beneath twinkling lights and falling snow, igniting a blend of excitement and uncertainty about what it means for their connection.

Chapter 6: His Smell (Noah's POV)

As Noah reflects on their first kiss, he can't shake the memory of Sienna's delicious vanilla-scented lotion that wafted toward him when they were together. He finds himself captivated by her beauty, her warm smile, and the sense of comfort and thrill he feels around her. At work, his colleagues tease him about having a 'girl crush' on Sienna, noticing how often he smiles when reading her messages or mentioning their plans.

Chapter 7: Her Taste (Sienna's POV)

After their kiss, Sienna goes home with a flurry of mixed emotions, feeling both giddy and apprehensive. Sharing the experience with her best friend over hot cocoa, she admits how thrilling yet daunting their connection feels. She recalls the thrill of the kiss, reliving the sweet taste of peppermint on Noah's lips, leaving her wondering if the magic of the moment could lead to something deeper.

Chapter 8: Internal Conflict/Resistance to Attraction (Noah's POV)

Despite the chemistry shared, Noah starts to retreat emotionally, overwhelmed by the intensity of his feelings for Sienna and fearing vulnerability. He worries that the depth of their connection could lead to heartache if it doesn't evolve as he hopes, thinking it's safer for both of them not to explore romance further. He debates whether he should prioritize focusing on his business instead of opening his heart again.

Chapter 9: Steamy Hot Intimate Scene (Sienna's POV)

On New Year's Eve, at Noah's gathering with friends, the atmosphere quickly heats up as they share close conversations, touches, and laughter. Noah pulls Sienna aside amidst the celebration, and they engage in a steamy kiss that escalates into a more intimate moment, leaving them both breathless. Their chemistry becomes undeniable, and they find themselves wrapped in each other's arms, losing track of time.

Chapter 10: Internal Falling in Love (Noah's POV)

As the days pass and the New Year dawns, Noah surprises himself by how deeply he feels for Sienna. She enters every thought, and he cherishes the laughter and warmth she brings into his life. Noah begins to see a future unfolding, imagining life with her filled with laughter, adventure, and shared dreams—a stark contrast to the solitude he previously felt.

Chapter 11: Dark Moment/Pulling Apart (Sienna's POV)

Tragedy strikes when an important life change occurs for Sienna, prompting her to reevaluate her priorities and future. Feeling distanced from Noah, she worries that their connection is too fresh to navigate a potential upheaval. Stressed and uncertain, she pulls away, believing it's for the best. Noah feels the sudden gap and is left confused and heartbroken, unsure of how to reach her.

Chapter 12: Resolution (Noah's POV)

Noah confronts his feelings and decides he can't lose Sienna without expressing his love. He makes an effort to reach out and understands her struggles. After a heartfelt conversation over coffee, she opens up about her fears, and together they discuss their aspirations, realizing they can support each other through challenges.

Noah demonstrates his commitment to fight for their relationship, and Sienna feels reassured.

Epilogue: HEA (Sienna's POV)

In the glow of the following Christmas season, Sienna and Noah are thriving together, both in love and in their respective passions. They continue to work through life's ups and downs hand-in-hand, co-managing Festive Faves. On Christmas Eve, they indulge in the festivities while creating new holiday traditions as a couple. As they stand beneath the twinkling lights, exchanging gifts, Noah presents Sienna with a heartfelt ornament symbolizing their love, and Sienna knows that her leap of faith led her to the most meaningful adventure of all—finding true love.

Outline for A Perfect Match

Chapter 1. Intro to Heroine

Heroine: Nora Lane - Nora Lane is introduced as a dedicated marketing executive intent on climbing the corporate ladder. In her small, meticulously organized apartment, she reflects on her childhood ambitions of becoming an artist and the chances she gave up in pursuit of success. Her skepticism toward love continues to grow after a recent breakup with a man who only cared about his reputation. She confides in a close friend, who encourages her to try out a trendy new matchmaking app.

Chapter 2. Intro to Hero

Hero: Ted Cole - Ted Cole, a laid-back barista and aspiring musician, talks about his love for art and music while feeling stuck in a dead-end job. He finds solace in playing his guitar at local open mic nights. Unlike Nora, he embraces spontaneity but feels disillusioned with romance after a bitter breakup. While closing up at the coffee shop, he mentions to his coworker that dating is not for him anymore, but he is reluctantly nudged to try the app by friends.

Chapter 3. Meet Cute

Heroine: Nora Lane - Nora gets matched on MatchMakers United just before a coffee break. Realizing she is meeting her match at her favorite local café, she imagines a dreamy encounter. When she arrives, excitement turns to dismay as she sees Ted, the barista who always gives her attitude about her coffee orders. Their banter escalates into a playful, competitive conversation.

Chapter 4. Growing Attraction/Getting to Know Each Other

Hero: Ted Cole - Ted battles his initial annoyance at Nora but can't help appreciating her fiery spirit. As they engage in more banter over drinks, their competitive nature keeps surfacing. He sees a fun dynamic forming, and when they accidentally brush hands, it ignites an unexpected spark of attraction. Despite their bickering, Ted begins to admire her ambition.

Chapter 5. First Kiss

Heroine: Nora Lane - Nora finds herself at an open mic night to support Ted, who is reluctantly performing. As he sings one of his original songs, she feels a rush of emotions wash over her. In a moment of spontaneity, they kiss after the performance, igniting an unexpected chemistry that surprises them both. Nora is left breathless, wondering if this could lead to something more.

Chapter 6. Her Smell

Hero: Ted Cole - Ted thinks of the lingering scent of Nora's floral perfume. He remembers how close they were that night and how it caught him off guard when he inhaled her scent for the first time. Confiding in his male coworker, he expresses confusion and excitement about his continuing connection with Nora, realizing he can't stop thinking about her smile and the spark they shared.

Chapter 7. His Taste - Heroine: Nora Lane

Nora reflects on the kiss, savoring the taste of Ted's coffee-kissed lips. Confiding in her closest friend over drinks, she shares how the kiss felt genuine and electric, yet overwhelming. She questions if it was just a moment or something deeper while battling the fear of falling into yet another unrequited romance.

Chapter 8. Internal Conflict/Resistance to Attraction

Hero: Ted Cole - Ted wrestles with his growing feelings for Nora and his fear of vulnerability. He wonders if he can really trust someone after being hurt. While talking to his best friend, he admits he's never felt this way about anyone. He also reflects on the pressures of Nora's world of marketing versus his laid-back lifestyle, leading him to question if they are truly compatible.

Chapter 9. Steamy Hot Intimate Scene - Heroine: Nora Lane

Nora and Ted's shift from banter to deeper intimacy comes to a head one evening when they find themselves alone in his apartment after a failed dinner date. As passion ignites, they share an intimate moment that propels their relationship to new heights. Nora feels liberated yet nervous, questioning where this intensity might lead.

Chapter 10. Internal Falling in Love - Hero: Ted Cole

In the days following their intimate night, Ted realizes he is falling for Nora. In moments of solitude, he reflects on how much she adds excitement and positivity to his life. He shares with his friend how he admires her determination in her career and how their connection feels both effortless and enriching.

Chapter 11. Dark Moment/Pulling Apart - Heroine: Nora Lane

Nora becomes overwhelmed when a big promotion opportunity arises at work, causing her to push Ted away. She worries that she risks getting distracted from her career goals if she allows her feelings to grow. Meanwhile, a misunderstanding occurs when Ted sees her engrossed in a meeting with her manager and assumes she's lost interest.

Chapter 12. Resolution - Hero: Ted Cole

Ted takes a step back, allowing Nora space, but finds it increasingly difficult to do so. Realizing that he can't let go, he decides to confront her about their feelings. Their emotional reunion leads to a heartfelt discussion about their fears and dreams, clearing the air and allowing them to understand the value of supporting each other in the pursuit of love and ambition.

Chapter 13. Epilogue with HEA - Heroine: Nora Lane

In the epilogue, Nora reflects on their journey together while preparing for a Valentine's Day event at the coffee shop, now a rightful partner to Ted. They have successfully integrated their worlds, and Ted prepares to perform after launching his music career. As Nora admires him from the audience, it becomes clear they have built a lasting love founded on mutual respect and appreciation. The crowd erupts in applause, and Ted's eyes meet hers, sealing their happily ever after with a lingering gaze full of promise.

Title: A Christmas to Remember

Chapter 1: Sophie's POV - Intro to Heroine

Sophie Miller is introduced as a warm-hearted, optimistic woman in her late twenties. As a freelance graphic designer, she thrives on creativity but struggles with feelings of loneliness during the holiday season. With Christmas just around the corner, her excitement is palpable, especially with Bella, her golden retriever, by her side. The story opens with Sophie preparing holiday decorations in her cozy apartment, reflecting on her desire for meaningful connections.

Chapter 2: Fynn's POV - Intro to Hero

Fynn Carter is introduced as a ruggedly handsome man in his early thirties, living in the same neighborhood as Sophie. He runs a successful local pet supply store but is feeling the weight of recent personal losses. Despite his career success, he grapples with loneliness and longings for deeper connections this holiday season. The chapter highlights Fynn's desire to find joy in simple moments, hinting at his fascination with community and animals.

Chapter 3: Meet Cute (Sophie's POV)

After Bella goes missing on Christmas Eve, Sophie's panic escalates as she searches the nearby streets while plastering flyers in hopes of finding her. Just as despair starts to set in, she encounters Fynn, who has noticed her flyers around his home. He gently comforts her and, after a brief exchange, offers to help her search, offering a ray of hope in the midst of her worry.

Chapter 4: Growing Attraction/Getting to Know Each Other (Fynn's POV)

During their search, Fynn starts to really notice Sophie. He admires her passion and determination, feeling drawn to her positivity amidst chaos. They engage in light-hearted conversation, sharing funny dog stories, and initial sparks of attraction begin to flicker. Fynn finds himself increasingly captivated by Sophie's light, feeling as though he has known her forever.

Chapter 5: First Kiss (Sophie's POV)

Later, after Fynn invites Sophie into his home to warm up and briefly escape the cold, they find Bella curled up next to the roaring fireplace. Overwhelmed with relief and gratitude, the warmth of the moment transcends into something deeper as they share a lingering look. In a spontaneous surge of emotion, they share a sweet but electrifying first kiss that leaves them both breathless, setting their hearts racing on that magical Christmas Eve.

Chapter 6: His Smell (Fynn's POV)

Fynn reflects on that magical kiss while tidying up his living space the next day. He recalls the lingering scent of Sophie's cinnamon perfume that filled the air, reminding him of her beauty, her laugh, and the warmth of her presence. He finds himself smiling as he remembers the way her hair smelled like winter—fresh and invigorating. A close friend visits him and teases him about Sophie, noticing how smitten he seems.

Chapter 7: Her Taste (Sophie's POV)

As Sophie enjoys her Christmas morning alone, she can't help but think back on the kiss and the tenderness of Fynn's lips. She recalls the sweetness of their moments together—the taste of the hot cocoa they shared blending with the emotions flooding her heart. Confiding in her best friend over a phone call, she expresses both excitement and apprehension about how quickly they've connected, marveling at the unexpected chemistry and the thrill of it all.

Chapter 8: Internal Conflict/Resistance to Attraction (Fynn's POV)

Despite his undeniable attraction to Sophie, Fynn wrestles with his vulnerability. Haunted by fears of getting hurt again, he pulls back emotionally, questioning if he should keep things casual. He worries that Sofie's bright spirit might eventually turn into a reminder of his own struggles and commitment issues, leading to an internal battle as he grapples with his feelings.

Chapter 9: Steamy Hot Intimate Scene (Sophie's POV)

After spending most of Christmas Day together, Fynn and Sophie find themselves in a cozy corner of his home, wrapped in holiday lights and laughter. Their chemistry culminates in a passionate moment, marked by tender embraces and whispers. They share a steamy kiss that ignites a deeper connection, and the night sweeps away all doubts as they revel in the joy of being together, making it a Christmas they will never forget.

Chapter 10: Internal Falling in Love (Fynn's POV)

As days turn into a week of shared moments, Fynn's feelings for Sophie grow stronger. He observes the way she interacts with other people, the tender way she cares for Bella, and how she inspires him. The uncertainties begin to fade, and he realizes he wants more than just a fleeting romance. He envisions a future together, feeling warmth blossom in his heart, but still battles with the risk of truly opening up.

Chapter 11: Dark Moment/Pulling Apart (Sophie's POV)

As New Year's approaches, Sophie unwittingly discovers rumors about Fynn's past that shake her trust—she learns that he has a history of distancing himself from relationships. In a moment of vulnerability, she voices her insecurities about their swift connection and the potential for heartbreak, inadvertently pushing him away. Fynn's fear of commitment resurfaces, leading to a misunderstanding that leaves them both feeling distant and heartbroken.

Chapter 12: Resolution (Fynn's POV)

Fynn rises to the challenge of proving his feelings for Sophie and confronts his internal conflicts. He reaches out to her and expresses how much she means to him, admitting his fear but also his desire to fight for their connection. They have an open-hearted conversation, clearing misunderstandings, and realizing they both deserve love—they agree to embrace the unknowns together.

Epilogue: HEA (Sophie's POV)

As one year wraps up and the New Year begins, Sophie and Fynn celebrate with Bella by their side. They reflect on the past month full of joy, love, and unexpected turns and step forward into their bright future together, exchanging small handmade gifts that symbolize their love. Surrounded by warmth, laughter, and their furry companion, they embrace the magic of the holidays and the beauty of their journey, now committed to one another as they embark on a brand new adventure together.

Title: The 12 Days of Christmas Secrets

Chapter 1: Jess's POV - Intro to Heroine

Jess Parker is introduced as a spirited and creative woman in her late twenties, brimming with the holiday spirit despite her recent breakup. She works as a graphic designer and values her close friendship with Belle, who is her confidante and biggest cheerleader. As the chapter unfolds, we see Jess's affectionate relationship with her dog, Max, and her desire for true love amidst the festive chaos around her.

Chapter 2: Belle's POV - Intro to Hero

Belle Johnson is introduced as a free-spirited and adventurous woman, also in her late twenties, who secretly harbors feelings for Jess. She's a baker and spends the holiday season creating decadent treats for their friends and local events. Belle is struggling with her emotions—wanting to express her love for Jess but fearing it could jeopardize their friendship. This chapter highlights Belle's penchant for creating surprises, setting the stage for her secret planner role.

Chapter 3: Meet Cute (Jess's POV)

On the first snowy morning of December, Jess is outside with Max, frustrated over a stubborn package she's trying to open. Belle appears, jokingly bantering with Jess as she expertly opens the package. Their playful teasing turns into laughter as they reminisce about childhood Christmases. Little do they know, this is where Belle's plan begins; she's motivated to make this season unforgettable for Jess through her thoughtful gifts.

Chapter 4: Growing Attraction/Getting to Know Each Other (Belle's POV)

As the first gift arrives, Jess can't contain her excitement and rushes to share it with Belle. The gifts create opportunities for both women to bond over their shared passions—whether it's discussing the significance of each gift or planning holiday activities. Belle internally acknowledges her growing feelings for Jess, even as Jess remains oblivious to the true meaning behind the gifts and their deeper connection.

Chapter 5: First Kiss (Jess's POV)

On Day 6, after Jess receives a particularly touching gift (a scrapbook filled with their shared memories), Belle suggests they take their holiday revelry to a local ice rink. Amidst laughter and playful skating, a moment presents itself where Jess looks into Belle's eyes and feels a spark. Belle, overwhelmed by her emotions, leans in, and they share a sweet, tentative first kiss. Jess is blown away by the warmth and affection she feels but brushes it off, misinterpreting her feelings as excitement over the holidays.

Chapter 6: Her Smell (Belle's POV)

As Belle reflects on their kiss while baking for a holiday party, she can't shake the scent of warm vanilla and cinnamon that seems to linger in her clothes from that night. Memories of Jess's laughter play in her mind, and she feels both exhilarated and conflicted. Belle's best friend, who is often supportive, notices her distracted demeanor and playfully teases her about her smitten behavior, prompting Belle to acknowledge her feelings.

Chapter 7: His Taste (Jess's POV)

Later that week, Jess confides in Belle about their kiss, admitting how unexpected and thrilling it was. Alone in her room, Jess highlights how sweet Belle's lips tasted, like the hot cocoa they had shared. She finds herself replaying the moment and feeling confused about her emotions, questioning whether their friendship can withstand the kiss. Jess expresses her admiration for Belle and her fear of what it might mean for their future.

Chapter 8: Internal Conflict/Resistance to Attraction (Belle's POV)

As the days progress, Belle wrestles with her decision to express her feelings. The gifts keep coming, deepening their bond, yet Belle worries that revealing her love for Jess might shatter their friendship. She contemplates whether to confess or retreat, feeling torn as the holidays provide both warmth and an opportunity for vulnerability. Belle's internal struggle gives readers insight into her profound love for Jess amid the joyous festivities.

Chapter 9: Steamy Hot Intimate Scene (Jess's POV)

On Christmas Eve, Jess hosts a small gathering at her apartment. Fueled by a mix of holiday spirit and the close proximity they share,

Jess and Belle find themselves alone in the kitchen. Surrounded by twinkling lights and holiday aromas, they become engulfed in a heat of the moment, sharing soft kisses that transition into more passionate exchanges. The boundaries are blurred, and for the first time, Jess allows herself to embrace the possibility of love with Belle.

Chapter 10: Internal Falling in Love (Belle's POV)

As Christmas Day approaches, Belle finds herself reflecting deeply on the beautiful moments they've shared, feeling completely in love with Jess. She acknowledges that their bond is transforming into something more and grapples with the idea of taking a leap of faith. Belle realizes that love can be both exhilarating and terrifying, but she wants nothing more than to explore this journey with Jess by her side.

Chapter 11: Dark Moment/Pulling Apart (Jess's POV)

On the following day, Jess learns that Belle had been the mystery gift-giver all along. Feeling deceived and confused, she confronts Belle, unsure if she can handle the complexity of romantic feelings layered within their friendship. Jess isolates herself, needing time to process the revelations. Belle feels heartbroken and regrets her decision to keep her feelings hidden, feeling the chasm grow between them.

Chapter 12: Resolution (Belle's POV)

Belle takes the initiative to reach out after a few days of silence. She arranges a heartfelt evening to talk things through, crafting an environment filled with comfort and honesty. Belle pours her heart out, expressing her true feelings and apologizing for any confusion. Jess listens intently, confronting her feelings and understanding the depth of Belle's love. With a mix of tenderness and vulnerability, they find their way back to one another, embracing the reality of their relationship.

Epilogue: HEA (Jess's POV)

In the New Year, Jess and Belle celebrate together—a newfound love igniting between them. They reflect on the past month with laughter, joy, and a couple of surprises in the form of gifts they exchange—a combination of humor and heartfelt tokens. Surrounded by their friends, Jess and Belle share a chaste kiss to ring in the New Year, solidifying their romantic connection. They express gratitude for the journey they've taken and embrace the magic of love blossoming in the festive spirit, ready to step forward together into their bright future.

Title: A Christmas Invitation

Chapter 1: Sarah's POV - Intro to Heroine

Sarah Ellis is a cheerful and warm-hearted woman in her late twenties, deeply connected to her family and rooted in holiday traditions. As Christmas approaches, she struggles with the recent dissolution of her long-term relationship, casting a shadow over her favorite time of year. Despite her sadness, she is determined to make the best of the holidays for her family, looking forward to the annual Christmas morning where they exchange gifts over bagels and coffee.

Chapter 2: Alex's POV - Intro to Hero

Alex Donovan, in his thirties, represents a contrasting presence to Sarah. He is a talented musician but finds himself stuck as a barista this Christmas, burdened by the weight of personal loss and a complicated past. Christmas feels like an empty reminder of his unmet dreams and the family he no longer has. Though he outwardly appears gloomy, deep down, he yearns for connection and healing, wishing for a different holiday experience.

Chapter 3: Meet Cute (Sarah's POV)

On Christmas morning, Sarah heads to her local coffee shop with excitement, eager to grab her usual order. She notices the new barista, Alex, with his brooding presence and seemingly detached demeanor. When her order is mixed up, Sarah playfully challenges Alex about his coffee-making skills. Their light banter breaks the ice, and Sarah feels an unexpected spark as she looks into his deep eyes, noticing his subtle vulnerability beneath his surface.

Chapter 4: Growing Attraction/Getting to Know Each Other (Alex's POV)

As Sarah begins to visit the café daily throughout the week leading up to Christmas, they engage in deeper conversations. Alex learns about Sarah's cherished family traditions, warmth, and determination to make the holidays special despite her recent heartache. He finds himself increasingly drawn to her, discovering that her laughter and spirit uplift him in ways he hasn't felt in years. Meanwhile, Sarah feels a strange comfort in Alex's presence, sensing a kindred spirit beneath his sadness.

Chapter 5: First Kiss (Sarah's POV)

On a particularly cozy evening, Sarah invites Alex to join her for a hot chocolate after his shift. Bathed in twinkling holiday lights, they share laughter and stories, the atmosphere electric with chemistry. As they stroll outside in the snow, Sarah leans in and, impelled by the moment, kisses Alex—soft and tentative at first, before they both let go. It's a rush of warmth that surprises her, but as they pull away, uncertainty blooms in the back of her mind about what this means for them.

Chapter 6: Her Smell (Alex's POV)

After their kiss, Alex can't shake the scent of Sarah—a sweet blend of cinnamon from her favorite holiday pastries and her floral perfume. At work, he finds himself daydreaming about her smile, laughter, and how warm it felt when their lips met. His coworker notices his distraction and teasingly calls him out, prompting Alex to finally admit he's been thinking about Sarah more than he should. He grapples with internal conflict: wanting to embrace these feelings but fearing the vulnerability that comes with it.

Chapter 7: His Taste (Sarah's POV)

In the comforting solitude of her home, Sarah reflects on the kiss with Alex and can't help but smile at the memory. She confides in her best friend over a phone call, speaking about how his kiss lingered with the sweetness of chocolate mingled with peppermint—intensifying her desires. Sarah wrestles with her thoughts, recognizing that she's falling for him but torn by the fear of moving too fast after her breakup.

Chapter 8: Internal Conflict/Resistance to Attraction (Alex's POV)

While embracing his budding feelings, Alex feels a resurgence of doubt about whether he's ready to open up again. Memories of past holidays spent with family, juxtaposed with the loneliness he feels, begin to clash with his hopeful feelings toward Sarah. He fights the inexplicable pull he feels toward her and considers stepping back to avoid further heartbreak. His internal struggle becomes acute, threatening the budding relationship with Sarah, who seems to have rekindled the holiday spirit in him.

Chapter 9: Steamy Hot Intimate Scene (Sarah's POV)

With each passing day, Sarah's feelings deepen, and during a cozy evening at her family home, she invites Alex to stay a little longer. After dinner, they retreat to the living room, engrossed in conversation only to find themselves wrapped up in each other's warmth. As they draw closer, there is a magnetic pull that envelops them, leading to a passionate exchange that ignites their romance in a flurry of excitement and intimacy, reinforcing the connection they had forged.

Chapter 10: Internal Falling in Love (Alex's POV)

As Christmas approaches, Alex's heartache begins to dissipate. Spending time with Sarah allows him to dream again—hoping to find healing through love. He reflects on the beauty of her spirit and their shared moments, realizing he's deeply in love for the first time in years. Despite the hesitation to fully commit, he knows he doesn't want to lose the happiness that comes from being with her, feeling more like himself and more hopeful than he has in ages.

Chapter 11: Dark Moment/Pulling Apart (Sarah's POV)

Just days before Christmas, as excitement builds, Sarah receives an unexpected phone call from an old acquaintance, stirring her emotions. She learns that her ex is trying to reconcile, leading her to question her feelings for Alex. In a moment of confusion, she accidentally communicates her doubts while discussing plans for Christmas with Alex, causing them to unintentionally drift apart. Alex feels the distance and wrestles with insecurity, fearing he would be abandoned yet again.

Chapter 12: Resolution (Alex's POV)

The day before Christmas, Alex decides he cannot let fear dictate his life any longer. He resolves to confront Sarah about the misunderstanding, eager to fight for their connection. When they finally meet, hearts laid bare, Alex expresses his feelings for Sarah and reassures her about his intentions, emphasizing the genuine love and hope they share. They work through their fears together, realizing they both face their pasts but can stand side by side to create a brighter future.

Epilogue: HEA (Sarah's POV)

On Christmas morning, Sarah awakens filled with warmth and the promise of love. Alex surprises her by showing up at her family's house with a festive bouquet and holiday pastries he made himself. Together, they partake in Sarah's family traditions, creating new memories while reinforcing their bond. Surrounded by family, laughter, and festive decor, Sarah and Alex share a sweet kiss, solidifying the happiness they've found together—an unexpected love blossoming amidst the Christmas spirit. The story closes with Sarah embracing her heart's desires, ready for the fulfilling future that awaits with Alex by her side.

Outline for Christmas Get Together

Chapter 1: Intro to Heroine (Kara's POV)

Kara Harris is introduced as a clever but insecure professional in her late twenties. Her parents are hosting their annual Christmas Eve party, and the pressure to bring a date weighs heavily on her. She reflects on her unlucky love life and how the holidays can amplify loneliness.

Chapter 2: Intro to Hero (Liam's POV)

Introducing Liam Thompson, an aspiring chef who is just coming out of a messy breakup. He's charming, witty, and passionate about cooking. While he's content with his small-town life, he struggles with his desire for deeper connections. The holiday season feels particularly isolating for him this year.

Chapter 3: Meet Cute (Kara's POV)

Kara's first date with a more traditional match at the dating service goes hilariously wrong when he spills hot cocoa all over her. Flustered but laughing, she stumbles into Liam at the nearby bookstore where he works. Their instant rapport sparks a glimmer of hope amid the dating chaos.

Chapter 4: Growing Attraction/Getting to Know Each Other (Liam's POV)

As they embark on their unconventional date—baking cookies together—Liam is dazzled by Kara's quirky sense of humor. Their chemistry builds, and they exchange personal anecdotes about their families, deepening their connection.

Chapter 5: First Kiss (Kara's POV)

On a snowy evening, while sharing a laugh over frosting technique, Liam leans in and kisses Kara unexpectedly. The surprise ignites a wonderful mix of thrill and vulnerability within her. They both feel a charge that makes them realize this is more than just a casual Christmas date.

Chapter 6: Her Smell (Liam's POV)

As Liam works at the restaurant, he finds himself daydreaming about Kara, reminiscing about the scent of fresh pine and sugar cookies that surrounded them when they kissed. His best friend teasingly remarks on how smitten he is with her, causing Liam to blush and wonder if his feelings are real.

Chapter 7: His Taste (Kara's POV)

Later, while confiding in her sister about the kiss, Kara can't help but smile. Replaying it in her mind, she recalls the warmth of Liam's lips and how his voice made her heart race. Emboldened by their connection, she feels a stirring sense of hope that maybe love isn't so elusive after all.

Chapter 8: Internal Conflict/Resistance to Attraction (Liam's POV)

Liam wrestles with the fear of falling for someone again after his recent breakup. He questions whether it's wise to pursue something deeper with Kara, fearing he might expose himself to hurt. He tries to keep a cool distance while still spending time with her.

Chapter 9: Steamy Hot Intimate Scene (Kara's POV)

During a cozy, candlelit dinner at Liam's place, the atmosphere thickens with undeniable tension. As they share stories and laughter, one intimate look leads to another, and they embrace in a passionate kiss that spills over into a night of warmth and connection.

Chapter 10: Internal Falling in Love (Liam's POV)

As December continues, Liam realizes he's fallen hard for Kara. He notices her quirks—the way she bites her lip when she's contemplating something—and finds comfort in sharing silent moments. He starts envisioning a future together, affording him a sense of joy he's been missing.

Chapter 11: Dark Moment/Pulling Apart (Kara's POV)

Just days before Christmas Eve, Kara overhears a conversation between Liam and his friend about how he doesn't believe in enduring relationships. Feeling insecure, she questions whether Liam truly sees her as anything but a temporary distraction and begins to withdraw emotionally.

Chapter 12: Resolution (Liam's POV)

Liam senses the change in Kara and, determined not to lose her, confronts her at the dating service's Christmas gathering. In a heartfelt confession, he admits his fears about relationships and reveals his genuine feelings for her. Together, they affirm that love is worth the risk.

Epilogue: HEA (Kara's and Liam's POV)

On Christmas Eve, Kara confidently walks into her family's party with Liam by her side. Together, they create a lasting impression, showcasing the strength of their love. Embracing the spirit of Christmas, they exchange thoughtful gifts, cementing their commitment to a future filled with shared holiday moments and love. The story closes with them sharing a soft kiss under the mistletoe, warmth radiating in the glow of twinkling lights, signifying a bright new beginning together.

Outline for A Secret of Snow

Chapter 1: Intro to Heroine (Jenna's POV)

Jenna Miller, a talented but introverted graphic designer at Crestwood Marketing, reflects on the annual holiday party. Overwhelmed by the pressure to fit in and mingled with colleagues she barely knows, Jenna feels like an outsider, wondering if this year will feel even lonelier than the last.

Chapter 2: Intro to Hero (Ryan's POV)

Introducing Ryan Carter, a quiet but observant accountant known for his analytical mind and dry humor. He's been working at Crestwood Marketing for several years and has harbored a secret crush on Jenna—from a distance. While he's uncertain about approaching her, this year's party feels like a chance to break free from his social shell.

Chapter 3: Meet Cute (Jenna's POV)

Jenna accidentally bumps into Ryan at the party while trying to escape a particularly cheesy game. As she apologizes and retakes her balance, they share an awkward moment where Jenna's nervous laughter eases the tension. Their conversation flows naturally amidst the chaos, igniting a flicker of interest in both of them.

Chapter 4: Growing Attraction/Getting to Know Each Other (Ryan's POV)

Throughout the party, Jenna and Ryan find themselves gravitating toward each other, bonding over shared interests in art and literature. Ryan is captivated by Jenna's vibrant personality and the warmth she displays when excited. He makes a mental note to find a way to keep their conversation going even after the party ends.

Chapter 5: First Kiss (Jenna's POV)

When the party wind down, Jenna is about to leave when she sees Ryan, who has stayed behind to help clean up. They share a tender moment, discussing their passions. Caught in the moment, Jenna feels bold and leans in to kiss him, feeling a rush of excitement and warmth.

Chapter 6: Her Smell (Ryan's POV)

As Ryan returns home, he can't shake off the scent of Jenna's floral perfume mingled with the fragrance of pine from the party. He thinks about her radiant smile and the way her laughter brightens the room. His best friend, knowing about Ryan's crush, playfully nudges him, pointing out that he has it bad for her, teasing him about needing to make a move.

Chapter 7: His Taste (Jenna's POV)

Later, while confiding in her sister about the kiss, Jenna relives the magic of the moment with Ryan. She can still feel the warmth of his lips and the depth of connection. Overjoyed, Jenna admits to her sister that she feels nervous and excited about pursuing something real with him for the first time.

Chapter 8: Internal Conflict/Resistance to Attraction (Ryan's POV)

Despite their budding connection, Ryan finds himself hesitating. Still shaken from his past failures in love, he grapples with the fear of vulnerability and the pain of rejection. He questions whether the risk of opening his heart is worth it, causing him to pull back emotionally from Jenna.

Chapter 9: Steamy Hot Intimate Scene (Jenna's POV)

After a few more dates filled with laughs, Jenna invites Ryan over for a cozy snow globe-themed dinner party at her apartment. As they cook and share stories, the atmosphere becomes charged with chemistry. One flirtatious glance leads to heated kisses and passionate embraces, deepening their connection in a beautiful, intimate moment.

Chapter 10: Internal Falling in Love (Ryan's POV)

As the days progress, Ryan finds himself falling deeply in love with Jenna. He senses it during casual conversations and shared laughter. The small things—her spontaneity, her kindness—make his heart swell. He realizes he wants to create a future with her and is reminded constantly of her.

Chapter 11: Dark Moment/Pulling Apart (Jenna's POV)

Just when everything seems perfect, Jenna overhears Ryan discussing his reservations about their relationship with a coworker. Misunderstanding his fears as a sign he is not serious about her, she feels heartbroken and withdraws, believing she has been foolish to hope for something lasting.

Chapter 12: Resolution (Ryan's POV)

Determined not to lose Jenna, Ryan confronts her at the office days later, explaining his fears and assuring her of his feelings. He reveals how difficult it was to open up but emphasizes that she is worth every risk. Their conversation paves the way for healing and understanding, as they agree to move forward together.

Epilogue: HEA (Jenna's and Ryan's POV)

Months later, Jenna and Ryan celebrate the end of the year at the same holiday party, now as a couple. They reminisce about the snowy beginnings of their love while standing under the mistletoe. With laughter and joy in their hearts, they exchange heartfelt gifts, including a custom-made snow globe that symbolizes their journey together. The story closes with them sharing a gentle kiss under the twinkling lights, surrounded by friends, fully embracing the magic of love and the season.

Outline for A Date Under the Lights

Chapter 1: Intro to Heroine (Penny's POV)

Penny Bennett is introduced as a dedicated event coordinator for the Rockefeller Center Christmas Tree lighting ceremony. As she navigates her busy office filled with students and volunteers, she reflects on the expectations surrounding this iconic event, feeling the pressure to make it perfect. Her meticulous nature and fierce work ethic are evident, but she harbors a longing for something more than just a successful career.

Chapter 2: Intro to Hero (Kellan's POV)

Kellan Price's character is revealed as a talented and charming performer who has struggled to find his footing in the music industry after gaining fame from a television singing competition. He's currently working at a local coffee shop, balancing his dreams of performing with the reality of bills to pay. Despite a charismatic exterior, Kellan feels a sense of disappointment and is searching for a way to reignite his passion for music.

Chapter 3: Meet Cute (Penny's POV)

Penny is in the midst of frantic last-minute preparations for the tree lighting event when she learns that her main performer has canceled. As she scrambles for a solution, she hears about Kellan's unexpected availability. She meets him at the café near Rockefeller Center, where they share a brief but electric exchange, instantly drawing the interest of both. Penny is surprised by how easy it is to connect with him, despite their different worlds.

Chapter 4: Growing Attraction/Getting to Know Each Other (Kellan's POV)

Kellan feels the spark when he meets Penny. He notices her determination and ambition, and it intrigues him. As they discuss the details of the event, Kellan is drawn to Penny's passion for her job and her commitment to making the ceremony a memorable experience. The tension builds as they share stories from their lives, learning about each other's dreams, fears, and backgrounds.

Chapter 5: First Kiss (Penny's POV)

After successfully securing Kellan as the last-minute performer, Penny invites him to join her for warm drinks in a quiet corner of the café after a hectic day of planning. As they talk and laugh, the chemistry becomes undeniable. Penny feels an unexpected urge and leans in, sharing a charged first kiss with Kellan that leaves them both breathless, setting the stage for something more profound.

Chapter 6: Her Smell (Kellan's POV)

The next day, Kellan can't shake the memory of Penny's scent—her mix of warm vanilla and fresh pine lingering in his mind. While he practices for the performance, and a coworker catches him smiling, they tease him about his obvious crush. Kellan's heart races at the thought of her, realizing how much he enjoys being around her and how rapidly he's falling for her.

Chapter 7: His Taste (Penny's POV)

Later, Penny confides in her best friend about the kiss with Kellan. She recalls the sweetness of his lips and the warmth that enveloped her. Her heart flutters as she relives the moment, filled with excitement and confusion about what it means for their relationship. Penny admits to feeling vulnerable but wonders if diving into romance during a crucial time could complicate everything.

Chapter 8: Internal Conflict/Resistance to Attraction (Kellan's POV)

Kellan wrestles with his growing feelings for Penny, realizing he could easily fall for her. He worries whether she's truly interested in him as more than a performer or if he's simply a convenience for her busy life. Fearing rejection and mindful of his past disappointments, Kellan debates if he should take a step back to protect his heart.

Chapter 9: Steamy Hot Intimate Scene (Penny's POV)

As the nights grow colder, Penny invites Kellan to help her set up for the tree lighting. They share intimate moments while decorating, brushing against each other and exchanging playful banter. The tension escalates, leading to a passionate make-out session, where Penny feels liberated and adventurous, fully embracing the connection between them.

Chapter 10: Internal Falling in Love (Kellan's POV)

Kellan, overwhelmed with emotion, acknowledges that he's falling in love with Penny. During rehearsals, he watches her dive wholeheartedly into her work and feels a deep admiration. He envisions their future together, discussing music, travel, and dreams, even as doubts linger about whether she could truly reciprocate his feelings or view him as just a temporary fling.

Chapter 11: Dark Moment/Pulling Apart (Penny's POV)

Tension arises when Penny receives an unexpected phone call regarding a once-in-a-lifetime career opportunity—an out-of-state job that would conflict with her plans with Kellan. Torn between her ambitions and her connection to Kellan, Penny panics and distances herself, fearing she must choose between love and success.

Chapter 12: Resolution (Kellan's POV)

On the night of the tree lighting ceremony, Kellan pours his heart into his performance, hoping Penny will see the sincerity in his actions. When Penny watches him on stage, she realizes how deeply she cares for him and follows her instincts. After the ceremony, they meet amidst the festive lights, where Penny finally confesses her feelings and promises not to let go of what they have built together, resolving to embrace love and ambition simultaneously.

Epilogue: HEA (Penny's and Kellan's POV)

Months later, Penny and Kellan celebrate Christmas together in Manhattan, with the Rockefeller Center Christmas Tree twinkling above them. They reflect on how their careers have blossomed—Kellan landing a record deal, Penny successfully planning multiple high-profile events. They are now a couple, ready to face new adventures together, fully embracing both their love and dreams, completing the holiday with a cozy kiss as snow falls softly around them.

Title: Snowstorm Romance

Chapter 1: Intro to Heroine - Jemma's POV

Jemma Lane, a spirited and independent woman in her late twenties, is introduced in her cozy apartment as she excitedly prepares to fly home for Christmas. Decked out in holiday cheer, she reflects on her close family ties and the joy of the holiday season. However, her plans take a sudden downturn when she receives the news that her flight has been canceled due to a snowstorm, leaving her feeling disappointed and stuck in the city during the holidays.

Chapter 2: Intro to Hero - Liam's POV

Liam Chen, a charismatic and easy-going delivery driver in his early thirties, is introduced as he navigates through the wintry streets of the city. Despite the chaos of the storm, he remains cheerful, reminiscing about his own family traditions and the bittersweet feelings that Christmas brings. He longs for a deeper connection and romantic adventure but struggles with the loneliness that sometimes accompanies his job, especially during the holidays.

Chapter 3: Meet Cute - Jemma's POV

As Jemma scrolls through festive TV movies in her apartment, her stomach growls. She decides to order Chinese food to lift her spirits. When Liam arrives with her order, the moment is playful and fraught with unexpected chemistry. Jemma's clumsy excitement makes Liam smile, and their first interaction highlights their contrasting personalities—her bubbly demeanor versus his calm confidence.

Chapter 4: Growing Attraction/Getting to Know Each Other - Liam's POV

After realizing that the storm will keep him at work longer than expected, Liam returns to check on Jemma by offering to share a meal while they wait for the snow to clear. Their conversation flows easily, revealing their shared love for cheesy holiday movies. They laugh and share personal stories—Jemma's hilarious family memories and Liam's funny mishaps as a delivery guy—revealing common ground and setting the stage for their growing attraction.

Chapter 5: First Kiss - Jemma's POV

As the evening wears on and the snow builds outside, Jemma and Liam find themselves inching closer together, their hands brushing against each other. The atmosphere transforms, and they share a tentative first kiss—sweet and tentative at first, then deepening into something more passionate, full of promise and magic. Jemma's heart races as she realizes this unexpected connection is unlike anything she's felt before.

Chapter 6: Her Smell - Liam's POV

After the kiss, Liam can't shake the memory of Jemma. He finds himself captivated not only by her beauty and spark but also by her unique scent—a warm blend of vanilla and holiday spices that lingers in his memory. At work, his coworker notices his dreamy expression and teases him about his newfound infatuation, prompting Liam to realize just how deeply he's fallen for Jemma in such a short time.

Chapter 7: His Taste - Jemma's POV

Back in her apartment, Jemma reflects on the kiss. It was electric, leaving her feeling exhilarated and nervous all at once. She confides in her best friend via phone, relaying the details of the night, and how Liam's kiss felt both warm and comforting. She wonders if this connection could blossom into something more, but doubts linger about whether she's ready to embrace this new romantic chapter.

Chapter 8: Internal Conflict/Resistance to Attraction - Liam's POV

As the snowstorm begins to clear, Liam wrestles with his feelings for Jemma. While he's enchanted by her, he worries about their very different lives and the fact that she might return to her old routine after the holidays. Unable to dismiss his fears, he maintains distance but finds it increasingly difficult to stay away from Jemma, who holds a magnetic pull on his heart.

Chapter 9: Steamy Hot Intimate Scene - Jemma's POV

With the storm still swirling outside, Jemma and Liam end up back together in her apartment for a movie marathon. Amidst the laughter and warmth, the tension reaches its peak again. Their attraction ignites into a steamy encounter where they explore each other's desires, sharing deep kisses and heartfelt touches. The moment envelops them in passion, reminding both of them that sometimes magic happens when you least expect it.

Chapter 10: Internal Falling in Love - Liam's POV

Liam can't deny his feelings any longer as he reflects on how much he enjoys Jemma's company and the joy she brings into his life. Moments spent together feel effortless, and he starts envisioning a life beyond this magical Christmas, making plans, and getting lost in dreams—each new thought reinforcing the weight of his heart and the possibility of a future together.

Chapter 11: Dark Moment/Pulling Apart - Jemma's POV

Just as Jemma feels ready to embrace her feelings for Liam and the prospect of future adventures, she receives a call from her family urging her to return home to a family gathering that night, reminding her of her previous commitments. Conflicted, she pulls away from Liam, unsure if she should take a leap of faith or reconnect with her familiar life. The heart-wrenching moment leads to a painful goodbye, leaving them both feeling lost.

Chapter 12: Resolution - Liam's POV

In the aftermath of their separation, Liam realizes that he can't let Jemma walk away so easily. He musters his courage and rushes to her family gathering, finding her surrounded by loved ones but feeling a sense of longing for what they shared. In a heartwarming confrontation, he professes his feelings for her, believing Christmas magic truly exists, and he's ready to embrace a relationship, regardless of the uncertainties. Jemma's heart swells, and she, too, recognizes what they have is special.

Epilogue with HEA - Jemma and Liam's POV

A year later, Jemma and Liam celebrate their first Christmas together. They decorate a small tree in her apartment and reminisce over their unique journey, laughing at the memory of that unforgettable snowstorm. Surrounded by friends and family, they share new holiday traditions, filled with love and warmth. As they exchange gifts, both knowing they're on the cusp of a beautiful future, Liam leans in to kiss Jemma, marking the joy of love found amid the winter storm—and a promise of many more Christmases to come together.

Title: The 12 Dates of Christmas

Chapter 1: Intro to Heroine - Whitney's POV

Whitney Mayfield is introduced as an upbeat but somewhat insecure woman in her late twenties navigating a bustling city during December. As she decorates her apartment in preparation for the holiday season, she reflects on her family's snobbish traditions and the loneliness she feels, especially knowing her family's annual Christmas

Eve party is approaching and that she'll show up without a date once again.

Chapter 2: Intro to Hero - Kieran's POV

Kieran Thompson is revealed as a charming and laid-back graphic designer in his thirties who has recently returned to his hometown after years of living in a big city. While he enjoys the comforts of his family's traditions, he has struggled with meaningful connections in his romantic life. Working freelance offers him flexibility but leaves him feeling isolated, especially during the holidays.

Chapter 3: Meet Cute - Whitney's POV

Whitney's first blind date through the Mistletoe Match service with a boisterous banker goes awry, leading her to escape to a local café. There, she bumps into Kieran, who is sketching holiday scenes while sipping coffee. Their initial encounter is filled with awkward charm, and Whitney reveals her date mishap, sparking a connection over their shared sense of holiday frustration.

Chapter 4: Growing Attraction/Getting to Know Each Other - Kieran's POV

While fooling around with different festive activities for the holiday season, Whitney and Kieran begin to run into each other more frequently. They share meals, and laughter, and discuss their dreams and disappointments. Kieran finds himself captivated by Whitney's zest for life, and he admires her efforts to push through her loneliness while she notices his artistic spirit and thoughtful nature.

Chapter 5: First Kiss - Whitney's POV

As their chemistry builds, Whitney and Kieran find themselves at a Christmas market, adorned with lights and festive cheer. An impromptu game leads to misshaped snowballs, and laughter fills the air. In a tender moment, under shimmering decorations, they share their first kiss amid the magic of the market—sweet, spontaneous, and full of promise, leaving both yearning for more.

Chapter 6: Her Smell - Kieran's POV

Kieran can't forget the scent of Whitney—a delightful mix of peppermint and cocoa that lingers in his thoughts. At work, brainstorming creative ideas for holiday projects, his coworkers tease him about his distracted demeanor. They spot his obvious crush on Whitney and jokingly prod him, making Kieran realize he's truly smitten as he daydreams about their next encounter.

Chapter 7: His Taste - Whitney's POV

Later, while reflecting on their kiss in the sanctuary of her cozy apartment, Whitney reveals her feelings to her sister during a phone call. The kiss was electric, making her heart race. She admits how tender Kieran's lips felt against hers and how she's not quite ready to let go of the excitement of what this newfound connection could mean, stirring hope and dread in equal measure.

Chapter 8: Internal Conflict/Resistance to Attraction - Kieran's POV

As the days go by, Kieran grapples with his fears of getting too involved. He starts to notice a pattern in his romantic life: just when he feels things are going well, he gets nervous and pulls back. He admires Whitney but also worries if he can handle the expectations that come from dating someone as vibrant as her, especially as he prepares for a scheduled blind date that shakes him.

Chapter 9: Steamy Hot Intimate Scene - Whitney's POV

Amidst a cozy evening spent decorating cookies with friends, Kieran stops by, and the atmosphere crackles with unresolved tension. When they share a secluded moment away from the group, their attraction ignites, leading to a passionate rendezvous in the warmth of her apartment. Thrust into the heat of the moment, they lose themselves in each other, marking a turning point in their relationship.

Chapter 10: Internal Falling in Love - Kieran's POV

As Christmas approaches, Kieran finds himself imagining a life with Whitney. He realizes he's genuinely falling for her, thinking of her laughter, spirit, and the way she lights up a room. He envisions them at family gatherings and future holiday festivities, feeling an excitement he hasn't felt in years. However, he quells his thoughts, worried about the complexity that a deeper relationship might entail.

Chapter 11: Dark Moment/Pulling Apart - Whitney's POV

After the steamy encounter, reality sets in for Whitney when she learns about Kieran's upcoming blind date through the service. Heartbroken and feeling betrayed, she withdraws, fearing that Kieran may not be as committed as she hoped, despite the chemistry they share. When Kieran tries to reach out, she hesitates, uncertain about taking a risk on a man who might still be playing the field.

Chapter 12: Resolution - Kieran's POV

In the last days leading up to Christmas Eve, Kieran confronts his feelings and decides he can't let Whitney slip away. He finds her at the café where they originally met and lays his heart on the line, explaining how much she means to him and that he has canceled his blind date, realizing that she is the one he truly wants to be with. With a heartfelt plea, he asks her to join him at her family's Christmas Eve party, promising that he's in it for the long haul.

Epilogue with HEA - Whitney and Kieran's POV

On Christmas Eve, Whitney and Kieran attend the family gathering together, proudly showing up as a couple. Surrounded by family and the spirit of the season, they embrace the chaos and warmth of the occasion. As the night unfolds, Whitney realizes that, despite the initial trepidation and misadventures of the season, she has found love unexpectedly. With Kieran by her side, they share laughter, warmth, and a kiss under the mistletoe—knowing they'll create cherished holiday memories together for years to come, signifying the magic of love and the joy of being together.

Outline for Christmas Chaos and Unexpected Cheer
Chapter 1: Intro to Heroine - Cassidy's POV

Cassidy Collins introduces herself as a bubbly, optimistic young woman experiencing the joyful jitters of her first Christmas in her new home. She shares her excitement with her best friend during a coffee catch-up about all the decorations she plans to buy and her aspiration to create the perfect festive atmosphere. Cassidy's personality, aspirations, and slight clumsiness are highlighted, leading her to grocery shop for festive treats while carefully imagining every whimsical ornament she wants to adorn her house.

Chapter 2: Intro to Hero - Max's POV

Max Turner is introduced as the charming, dedicated manager of Wondrous Wonders, the local decor shop. He is shown juggling his responsibilities while preparing for the busy holiday season. Caring and slightly quirky, he has a reputation for going above and beyond for customers, even as he's secretly nursing a heartwarming but chaotic work environment. His inner thoughts reveal his appreciation for the magic of Christmas and a desire for connection, even if life has kept him busy and somewhat solitary.

Chapter 3: Meet Cute - Cassidy's POV

Cassidy finally arrives at Wondrous Wonders, excited and a little overwhelmed by the sheer amount of decorations available. During her enthusiastic expedition, she accidentally knocks over a shelf, causing an avalanche of ornaments to crash around her. Max, witnessing the disaster, rushes over to help. Their eyes meet—Cassidy feels both embarrassed and intrigued while Max fights to suppress a laugh. He offers assistance while embodying the holiday spirit, making the moment awkwardly charming.

Chapter 4: Growing Attraction/Getting to Know Each Other - Max's POV

Max takes a liking to Cassidy, finding her enthusiasm infectious despite the chaos she created. As they clean up together, they engage in playful banter, discovering shared interests in food and music. Max learns that she has a passion for sustainable living and making others smile. He observes her quirks and how she effortlessly disarms his initial frustration, stirring a mix of admiration and attraction in him—a realization he's not quite prepared for.

Chapter 5: First Kiss - Cassidy's POV

After several visits to the store and getting to know each other, Cassidy faces the Christmas rush and an opportunity to surprise Max with homemade cookies at the shop. The moment is filled with laughter and flour dust, and when an awkward shift leads them to lean in too close, they share a quick but powerful kiss. Cassidy feels a rush of warmth and disbelief as her cheeks flush—she's confused yet thrilled by the sudden shift in their relationship.

Chapter 6: Her Smell - Max's POV

In the days following their kiss, Max can't shake off the lingering memory of Cassidy's scent—cinnamon and pine mixed with a hint of her natural fresh fragrance. He often finds himself lost in thought, recalling her radiant smile and infectious laughter. His coworkers take notice of his distracted demeanor and tease him, raising his cheeks in warmth as he tries to downplay his growing feelings for Cassidy while internally acknowledging he's smitten.

Chapter 7: His Taste - Cassidy's POV

Reflecting on their kiss while making her own holiday treats, Cassidy confides in her sister over the phone about her unexpected romance with Max. She retells the moment, her heart racing as she remembers the warmth and sweetness of his lips. Cassidy realizes that the kiss meant more than a holiday fling—it captured her feelings that are blossoming into something deeper and unexpected, leaving her both excited and apprehensive.

Chapter 8: Internal Conflict/Resistance to Attraction - Max's POV

Max's feelings for Cassidy deepen, but he battles with a fear of pursuing a romance during such a hectic time. He questions whether he's ready for a relationship, fearing it might complicate his life and responsibilities. At a staff gathering, he witnesses Cassidy interact with customers effortlessly, making him realize that he can't hide from his feelings any longer. Still, he hesitates, thinking he might ruin her holiday spirit with his conflicting commitments.

Chapter 9: Steamy Hot Intimate Scene - Cassidy's POV

After a long day at the shop, Max invites Cassidy for a cozy hot chocolate at his favorite local café. As they sit close, laughter and playful touches transform into undeniable chemistry. They share stories and laughter, gradually slipping into a more intimate atmosphere as Christmas carols fill the air. When they head back to Max's place to admire the decorations he's working on, the tension culminates in a heated makeout session that leaves them breathless.

Chapter 10: Internal Falling in Love - Max's POV

As the holiday draws closer, Max finds himself spiraling into deep feelings for Cassidy. He treasures the moments they've shared, and their mutual adventures around town highlight their compatibility. With every laugh, each touch, he realizes Cassidy fills an emotional void he didn't know he had. While decorating together, he mentally commits to embracing a new start with her, thinking of plans for their future, infusing him with warmth and hope.

Chapter 11: Dark Moment/Pulling Apart - Cassidy's POV

After inadvertently seeing Max discussing next season's sales forecasts and his busy schedule with a coworker, Cassidy feels insecure. She misinterprets his focus on work as disinterest in their blossoming relationship. Convinced she is just a temporary distraction, she pulls away, deciding to devote herself to her holiday preparations rather than pursue a romance that may lead nowhere. The tension between them thickens, and confusion clouds their once bright bond.

Chapter 12: Resolution - Max's POV

Max, confused and disheartened by Cassidy's withdrawal, decides to confront her. He shows up at her house with a heartfelt apology and a barrage of colorful Christmas decorations. Together, they unpack their feelings, revealing their fears and misunderstandings. Max expresses how she's the light in his chaotic life and how important she is to him, dispelling the fog that had formed between them. Cassidy's heart softens as they embrace the earnestness of their emotions.

Epilogue with HEA - Cassidy's POV

Months later, Cassidy and Max are happily decorating their shared home, reminiscing over their chaotic beginnings at Wondrous Wonders. Their love deepens as the holiday spirit surrounds them, and they make plans to throw a Christmas party for family and friends, inviting everyone to celebrate the beautiful chaos that their lives have become together. Cassidy reflects on how a little accident and a lot of heart brought them together, marking the beginning of many more holiday adventures to come as they hold hands and decorate their first tree as a couple, surrounded by love and laughter.

Enemies to Lovers & Second Chances

Outline for Reunion Sparks

Chapter 1: Intro to Heroine (Emily's POV)

Emily Sullivan is introduced as a successful but somewhat introverted author who struggles with her past insecurities from high school. She reflects on her childhood while preparing for her ten-year high school reunion, recalling her awkward teenage years and her fierce rivalry with James Thompson, the charismatic boy who teased her endlessly yet sparked a curious mix of feelings.

Chapter 2: Intro to Hero (James's POV)

James Finmore is introduced as a charming entrepreneur who has returned to Everwood with a successful business venture under his belt. Despite his outward confidence, he feels the weight of regret for some of his past behavior. As he prepares for the reunion, he reflects on his childhood and the heated rivalry with Emily, wondering what it might be like to see her again.

Chapter 3: Meet Cute (Emily's POV)

At the reunion, Emily steps into the lively hall and immediately spots James across the room. Their eyes meet, and a rush of adrenaline surges through her. When she accidentally bumps into him while trying to get a drink, she spills her soda all over his shirt. The ensuing playful banter reignites their competitive spirits, leaving both feeling unexpectedly exhilarated.

Chapter 4: Growing Attraction/Getting to Know Each Other (James's POV)

Throughout the evening, James is drawn to Emily's newfound confidence. As they navigate old acquaintances and reminisce about mutual childhood experiences, he starts to see her in a new light. Their conversations become deeper and more personal, sparking a chemistry that neither can ignore, despite their playful teasing.

Chapter 5: First Kiss (Emily's POV)

After the reunion, the event continues at a local pub. Under the dim lights and with laughter surrounding them, Emily and James engage in a lively debate about their high school days. The tension reaches a peak when James, feeling bold, leans in and kisses Emily softly, catching her off guard but igniting a fire within her that she had never recognized before.

Chapter 6: Her Smell (James's POV)

As James tries to process the kiss, he spends the day reflecting on Emily and how beautifully she had transformed. He recalls her scent—a delicate mix of jasmine and vanilla. This memory lingers in his mind and heightens his desire for her. Confiding in his best friend, he admits how much he admires her and grapples with feelings he never thought he'd have for his former rival.

Chapter 7: His Taste (Emily's POV)

Alone in her apartment, Emily reflects on their kiss. She can't shake the warmth that coursed through her when James's lips met hers; it was tantalizing and filled with a sense of longing. Her sister calls, and Emily confides in her about the surprising emotions she's experiencing, expressing both excitement and trepidation about what this means for their newfound connection.

Chapter 8: Internal Conflict/Resistance to Attraction (James's POV)

Despite the undeniable chemistry between them, James struggles with his guilt over his past treatment of Emily. He questions whether he deserves to pursue her and grapples with his commitment issues. During a conversation with his business mentor, he reveals his confusion and fears about rekindling a relationship with Emily, worried about potentially hurting her again.

Chapter 9: Steamy Hot Intimate Scene (Emily's POV)

During a weekend art festival, the two share a spontaneous moment at Emily's art exhibit. Surrounded by the vibrant colors and scents, their chemistry ignites once more, leading to an intimate scene filled with laughter and passion. They share heated kisses that envelop them in desire and assurance, pulling down the walls they had built around their hearts.

Chapter 10: Internal Falling in Love (James's POV)

As they spend more time together, James realizes that he is genuinely falling for Emily. He catches himself daydreaming about their future, feeling a sense of comfort and joy he hasn't felt in years. One night under the stars, he confides his feelings, realizing that part of him wants to make up for the past and be the man Emily deserves.

Chapter 11: Dark Moment/Pulling Apart (Emily's POV)

After confessing their feelings, a revelation about James's past and his reasons for teasing her in high school resurfaces, leaving Emily feeling vulnerable. An argument erupts, causing Emily to pull away, feeling conflicted by her feelings of betrayal and hurt. She worries whether their bond is built on a fragile foundation and retreats into herself, leaving James confused and heartbroken.

Chapter 12: Resolution (James's POV)

Determined to win Emily back, James sets out to prove that their love is more than just a chance at rekindling an old rivalry. He reaches out to her, explaining how he's changed and wants to build a future together. In a heartwarming confrontation at her favorite coffee shop, he pours his heart out, promising to cherish her and grow with her.

Epilogue with HEA

Months later, Emily and James are seen volunteering together at a local community project, laughter and love evident in their interactions. They have found their rhythm as a couple, successfully blending their lives and supporting each other's dreams. With warm smiles and playful banter, they reflect on their journey from childhood rivals to the greatest love story, sealed with a passionate kiss as they look toward their bright future together.

Outline for The Homecoming

Chapter 1: Intro to Heroine (Mila)

- Mila's perspective: Mila arrives back in Cedar Falls, reflecting on her past sports career and the unexpected end of her dreams. She reminisces about her high school days, filled with optimism, and feels a mix of nostalgia and regret as she pulls into her childhood home.

Chapter 2: Intro to Hero (Ryder)

- Ryder's perspective: Introduced as a hardworking mechanic with a strong sense of duty. He reflects on his own journey after high school, including the heartbreak of losing Mila. He's now a single father to a spirited young daughter, and he feels a void where love once thrived.

Chapter 3: Meet Cute

- Mila's perspective: As Mila walks through the local farmer's market, she unexpectedly bumps into Ryder. The encounter is awkward yet filled with unspoken emotions. Flashbacks of their high school romance flood her mind, and she struggles to read his reaction.

Chapter 4: Growing Attraction/Getting to Know Each Other

- Ryder's perspective: He recalls how he's always admired Mila's strength and determination. Despite his reluctance, he's drawn to the changes in her demeanor as she works at the market. They start running into each other more frequently, sharing casual conversations that open doors to memories.

Chapter 5: First Kiss

- Mila's perspective: During a small town event, they share a dance filled with a past connection and undeniable chemistry. Surrounded by laughter and friends, in a moment of vulnerability, Mila leans in and they share their first kiss, reigniting feelings long buried.

Chapter 6: Her Smell

- Ryder's perspective: As Ryder wraps his arms around Mila during a late evening stroll, he inhales her familiar scent—a mix of floral notes and fresh air. He realizes how deeply he's missed being close to her, evoking memories of their teenage love and what could again blossom.

Chapter 7: His Taste

- Mila's perspective: Mila reflects on how the taste of Ryder's kiss awakens a sense of longing in her. It's sweet and nostalgic, filling her heart with emotions she thought she'd buried. She begins to confront her feelings of doubt and the fear of risking another heartache.

Chapter 8: Internal Conflict/Resistance to Attraction

- Ryder's perspective: He wrestles with his feelings for Mila, reminding himself of the painful memories associated with their past. As much as he wants to embrace their rekindled romance, he fears putting his heart on the line again—for himself and his daughter.

Chapter 9: Steamy Hot Intimate Scene

- Mila's perspective: A heated moment in Mila's home leads to a night of passion. They explore their emotions and physicality, enveloped by the warmth of renewed love. It's a blend of intimacy and vulnerability that strengthens their bond, yet leaves them both wondering about the future.

Chapter 10: Internal Falling in Love

- Ryder's perspective: Post-intimacy, he can't shake off the overwhelming realization that he is falling for Mila. He recalls past conversations with his daughter about love and starts to entertain the idea of Mila becoming a part of their lives once more.

Chapter 11: Dark Moment/Pulling Apart

- Mila's perspective: Just as Mila begins to feel secure in their relationship, her insecurities resurface, fueled by fears of inadequacy and risk of rejection. An argument ensues when she brings up her issues, leading to conflicting emotions. She decides to pull back, leaving Ryder heartbroken.

Chapter 12: Resolution

- Ryder's perspective: Realizing the depth of his feelings, Ryder takes a step back to reflect and regroup. He reaches out to Mila, confronting her fears head-on and sharing his own. They have an emotional conversation that allows them both to express their vulnerabilities, leading to an agreement to face their challenges together.

Epilogue: Happy Ever After (HEA)

- Mila and Ryder, dual perspective: Several months later, Mila and Ryder stand together at the opening of an art exhibit showcasing Mila's work, inspired by their journey. Surrounded by friends and family, they celebrate their newfound love, gratitude, and the beautiful life they're building with Ryder's daughter, embracing the joys of family and love in Cedar Falls.

Outline for Old Friends

Chapter 1: Intro to Heroine (Brooke Carter)

- Brooke's Perspective: The story begins with Brooke, a dedicated high school teacher in Cedar Bluff, juggling her career and responsibilities. She reflects on her life's trajectory since high school—her passion for education, her close-knit circle of friends, and the lingering bitterness over her fallout with Bryan. Her thoughts reveal her deep-seated fears about reopening old wounds and the vulnerability that comes with reconnecting with someone she once loved.

Chapter 2: Intro to Hero (Bryan Thompson)

- Bryan's Perspective: Bryan, now a successful architect, returns to Maplewood after years in the bustling city. He feels the weight of his return, burdened by memories of his youth and the unresolved issues with Brooke. The narrative outlines his determination to make a mark in the town he once called home and how his past relationship with

Brooke shapes his emotional landscape, revealing a guilty conscience and hopes for reconnection.

Chapter 3: Meet Cute

- Brooke's Perspective: At the high school reunion, chaos ensues as Brooke spills her drink in front of a group of alums. As mortification overwhelms her, Bryan swoops in to help, and when their eyes meet, a flood of memories rushes back. Their interaction is laden with tension and unspoken words; it sets the stage as they both try to navigate their feelings while confronting decades-old history.

Chapter 4: Growing Attraction/Getting to Know Each Other

- Bryan's Perspective: Bryan is surprised by how easily he falls back into conversations with Brooke, reminiscing about their past and discovering the adult version of her. He admires whether she's grown into someone even more amazing than he remembers. Their interactions become lighter, as they begin to connect through shared interests and laugh over inside jokes, reigniting a spark they thought extinguished.

Chapter 5: First Kiss

- Brooke's Perspective: Following a shared moment of vulnerability, Brooke impulsively kisses Bryan in a secluded spot after the reunion party. The kiss is electric, a mix of regret from the past and promise for the future. Brooke pulls back, overwhelmed with emotions, and they both realize that despite the years apart, the chemistry is still palpable—and perhaps even stronger than before.

Chapter 6: His Taste

- Brooke's Perspective: After the kiss, Brooke is flooded with confusion and excitement. Later, she confides in her close friend Sarah about the kiss with Bryan. She describes how thrilling it felt and how it sent warmth flooding through her. In doing so, she realizes she's not just drawn to his looks but also his kindness and laughter. Sarah encourages her to explore these feelings, sensing that something meaningful is blossoming.

Chapter 7: Her Smell

- Bryan's Perspective: As Bryan goes about his daily routine, he can't shake the scent of Brooke that lingers in the air long after their kiss. The sweet aroma of vanilla and lavender reminds him of her beauty, her warm smile, and the depth of her eyes. During a casual lunch with a coworker, his friend notices Bryan's distracted state and comments that he must really be into someone, teasing him about his dreamy smile whenever he thinks of Brooke.

Chapter 8: Internal Conflict/Resistance to Attraction

- Bryan's Perspective: Bryan grapples with his growing feelings for Brooke, torn between wanting to pursue something deeper and the fear of ruining their rekindled friendship. The ghosts of their past still haunt him, leading him to push away thoughts of a romantic relationship, believing it might lead to heartbreak again. He wrestles with whether to unleash these emotions or to keep them bottled up.

Chapter 9: Steamy Hot Intimate Scene

- Brooke's Perspective: With the tension mounting, Brooke and Bryan share a passionate night together after a community event. The energy ignites an undeniable intimacy, blending vulnerability with longing. Both shed the emotional armor they've donned, diving headfirst into the connection that has been long overdue. The passion pulls them closer, intensifying their emotional bond and leaving them both breathless and uncertain about what comes next.

Chapter 10: Internal Falling in Love

- Bryan's Perspective: After their intimate night together, Bryan begins to realize he is falling in love with Brooke. Every moment spent with her feels like a rediscovery—he sees her strength and beauty in a new light. He reflects on how their relationship has evolved and how she challenges him to be a better man, beckoning him to let go of the past and embrace a fresh start.

Chapter 11: Dark Moment/Pulling Apart

- Brooke's Perspective: Just as things begin to solidify, Brooke overhears a conversation suggesting Bryan might not have been fully committed to the idea of staying in Maplewood. Feeling insecure and afraid of once again being heartbroken, she pulls away from him, convinced their romance will not withstand the pressure of reality. Bryan is left confused and heartbroken, desperate to make her see.

Chapter 12: Resolution

- Bryan's Perspective: Bryan, frustrated by Brooke's withdrawal, decides to confront her. He pours his heart out, confessing his love and acknowledging the past mistakes that haunted them both. They have an honest conversation about their insecurities, reinforced by the depth of their feelings. Each offers a heartfelt apology for the misunderstandings and fears, solidifying their commitment to moving forward together.

Epilogue: Happy Ever After (HEA)

- Brooke and Bryan's Perspectives: The story concludes with a glimpse into their future happier and healthier, sharing a cozy moment at their favorite coffee shop, discussing plans to renovate an old community center together. They reflect on how far they've come since the reunion, thankful for the second chance they fought for. The gentle touch of their hands and shared laughter seal their commitment to love, friendship, and a life filled with promise.

Outline for Home Court with POVs

Chapter 1: Intro to Heroine (Mira) - Mira's POV

Mira Dawson reflects on her life in the neighborhood where she grew up. Working as a caring social worker, she embodies strength and resilience but is haunted by memories of childhood struggles and the grief of losing her father. She longs for the joy she had during those carefree days spent with her best friend, Tyler, who seemed to vanish into the spotlight of fame. Her routines feel mundane, and she can't shake the feeling that a piece of her heart is still tethered to those childhood adventures.

Chapter 2: Intro to Hero (Tyler) - Tyler's POV

Tyler Brooks, now a celebrated basketball star, sits alone in his lavish mansion, feeling an emptiness beneath the glittering surface of his life. While he thrives professionally, his heart aches with the weight of his father's recent death and the growing distance from his childhood neighborhood—the one that taught him humility and connection. He grapples with the loneliness of fame and the raw pain of losing his father, as his mother urges him to return home for the funeral, stirring complex feelings of nostalgia and regret.

Chapter 3: Meet Cute - Mira's POV

As Tyler arrives at the old neighborhood, Mira is helping to organize the community's memorial for their late friend. When she unexpectedly bumps into Tyler on the street, a rush of childhood memories floods her mind. Their playful banter feels instantly familiar, yet there's a strange tension in the air. Mira is captivated by the glimmer of recognition in Tyler's eyes, and she's reminded of the bond they once shared. It feels both exhilarating and unsettling to see him again.

Chapter 4: Growing Attraction/Getting to Know Each Other - Tyler's POV

With Tyler back in town, he feels a magnetic pull toward Mira. Their interactions are vibrant and laced with laughter, but he can't ignore the whispers of his heart urging him to remember where he came from. With each encounter, he re-discovers Mira's warmth and strength, and he feels a longing that he thought he had buried beneath the layers of fame. He admires her passion for her work as a social worker and feels guilty for having left it all behind.

Chapter 5: First Kiss - Mira's POV

During a nighttime stroll through the neighborhood—a place filled with cherished memories—Mira finds herself opening up to Tyler about her grief and struggles. The conversation deepens their connection, and when Tyler leans in to kiss her, it feels like a culmination of all their past emotions. Mira's heart races as the kiss awakens something within her—something she hadn't allowed herself to feel in years. The moment is electric, leaving her breathless and confusingly happy.

Chapter 6: Her Smell - Tyler's POV

After the kiss, Tyler can't help but replay the moment in his mind, consumed by thoughts of Mira. Her scent lingers in the air—a sweet, citrusy reminder of simpler times. At practice, he zones out, daydreaming about her, leading a teammate to tease him about being lovesick. Tyler laughs it off, but internally, he struggles with feelings he hadn't anticipated. His heart is drawn to Mira, and he can't ignore just how much he desires to be close to her.

Chapter 7: His Taste - Mira's POV

Later, Mira cannot shake the memory of their kiss and finds herself confiding in her best friend about her feelings for Tyler. She describes the warmth of his lips and the shock of electricity that coursed through her. Her friend encourages her to embrace this new possibility, but Mira is torn between elation and fear of heartbreak. She reminisces about her childhood hopes with Tyler and questions whether it's wise to dive back into a relationship with someone whose life has skyrocketed beyond her reach.

Chapter 8: Internal Conflict/Resistance to Attraction - Tyler's POV

As days pass, Tyler feels an increasing internal conflict. He finds himself caught between the allure of Mira and the guilt of his past—how could he love someone from the old neighborhood while being celebrated for his present? He fears disappointing her and grapples with the prospect of leaving if his career demands it. As he tries to maintain a facade of confidence, doubts creep in, and he becomes more guarded, unsure how to navigate their deepening connection.

Chapter 9: Steamy Hot Intimate Scene - Mira's POV

After a day filled with poignant memories of Tyler's father, Mira and Tyler find comfort in each other. Surrounded by the ghosts of their childhood, they connect on an intense emotional level. Overwhelmed with vulnerability, they share a passionate encounter. Mira savors every moment—the way Tyler touches her, how he makes her feel cherished and desired. It's a whirlwind of raw emotion that leaves them both breathless and yearning for more.

Chapter 10: Internal Falling in Love - Tyler's POV

In the days following their intimate encounter, Tyler finds himself falling deeper for Mira. Her laughter, her kindness, and the way she inspires him to be better—it all weaves a spell over him that he cannot ignore. Tyler begins to understand that true fulfillment lies within love and connection, not just in fame or achievements. He contemplates how he wants to actively integrate Mira into his life, but fears the compatibility of their worlds.

Chapter 11: Dark Moment/Pulling Apart - Mira's POV

When Tyler confides that he has a potential deal to move across the country, the ground beneath Mira shifts. The spark they cultivated feels threatened. Mira's anxieties about being left behind resurface, and they argue about their different lives. In that heated moment, old wounds open, revealing her insecurities. Mira retreats, convinced that she cannot risk her heart if Tyler is destined for more than she can offer.

Chapter 12: Resolution - Tyler's POV

Heartbroken, Tyler spends reflective moments in the neighborhood that shaped him. He realizes that fame means little without the emotional tether he has to Mira. He gathers his courage and returns to her, ready to express his feelings genuinely. When he finds her—vulnerable yet strong—he knows they can create a life together that honors both their pasts and dreams. Tyler begs for another chance, and they share a moment of raw honesty, reclaiming what they thought was lost.

Epilogue with HEA - Mira's POV

Months later, with the neighborhood blooming with community projects, Mira finds herself thriving both personally and professionally alongside Tyler. He juggles his basketball career while supporting their shared philanthropic endeavors in the neighborhood. As they stand together at the opening of a new community center, they share an intimate kiss, knowing they've built a future intertwined with love, growth, and the nostalgic joy of rekindling a childhood bond. Their story is a testament to the power of roots and the magic of love that stands the test of time.

Outline for Finding the Beauty Within

Chapter 1: Intro to Heroine (Olivia's POV)

Olivia Hart sits in her cozy studio, surrounded by her colorful paintings that reflect her vibrant personality. As she works on a piece for an upcoming gallery show, memories of her childhood with Kaden flood her mind. She recalls their days spent in the small town of Willow Creek, feeling grateful for his unwavering support and companionship during her awkward adolescent years. Despite her growth and transformation, a lingering affection for Kaden remains, though she's unsure how to reconnect with him after all this time.

Chapter 2: Intro to Hero (Kaden's POV)

Kaden Mitchell has built a successful life as a tech entrepreneur in a bustling city, far removed from the small-town life he once knew. As he prepares for his return to Willow Creek for a visit, he reflects on his high school years spent as an outsider, the self-proclaimed nerd of the group. While excited to reunite with old friends, he can't help but think of Olivia—the girl who always saw him for who he truly was, and the one person he hopes to reconnect with one day.

Chapter 3: Meet Cute (Olivia's POV)

On the day of Kaden's return, Olivia is in town helping set up for the annual Willow Creek festival. When she bumps into Kaden at the local café, time seems to stand still. He is no longer the scrawny boy from high school, but a handsome, charismatic man. Their initial conversation is filled with playful banter and nostalgia, though Olivia feels a flutter of nervousness. Kaden can't help but admire the woman Olivia has become—confident and beautiful.

Chapter 4: Growing Attraction/Getting to Know Each Other (Kaden's POV)

As their paths cross more frequently during the festival, Kaden finds himself drawn to Olivia's newfound confidence and artistic spirit. They share laughter, reminisce about their childhood adventures, and enjoy exploring the festival together. Kaden realizes his admiration for her has turned into something deeper, while Olivia begins to see glimpses of the caring man beneath Kaden's charming exterior, igniting an undeniable spark between them.

Chapter 5: First Kiss (Olivia's POV)

Late one evening, as they walk through a quiet park after the festival, the atmosphere shifts. Surrounded by the whispers of nature, Olivia feels the weight of their connection and can no longer ignore her emotions. As they share stories and laughter, she unexpectedly leans in and kisses Kaden softly. The kiss is tender yet electrifying, confirming the feelings they have been dancing around. When they pull away, Olivia is filled with joy and anxiety, questioning what this means for their relationship.

Chapter 6: Her Smell (Kaden's POV)

Unable to shake off the memory of their kiss, Kaden is hit by the intoxicating scent of Olivia—an alluring mix of fresh paint and jasmine. He becomes more aware of her presence, longing to be close while feeling the weight of his past insecurities. When a close friend notices Kaden's distracted state, they tease him about having it bad for Olivia, leaving him flustered yet secretly elated. The teasing reminds him just how true his feelings for her are.

Chapter 7: His Taste (Olivia's POV)

Later that night, Olivia confides in her best friend about the kiss with Kaden. She recalls the taste of his lips—sweet and warm—and how it made her heart race. While gushing about their connection, Olivia feels a mix of excitement and fear. She's never been in love before, and the intensity of her feelings for Kaden is overwhelming. As she contemplates the kiss, she wonders if this is the beginning of something transformative or if she should pull back to protect herself.

Chapter 8: Internal Conflict/Resistance to Attraction (Kaden's POV)

Despite the thrill of their newfound intimacy, Kaden's insecurities resurface. Doubts creep in about whether he deserves Olivia's affection after all those years spent feeling out of place. He hesitates to fully commit, concerned that their blossoming romance could complicate their friendship or eventually lead to heartbreak. The dichotomy of wanting to explore this relationship while fearing rejection creates tension within him, pushing him to create distance.

Chapter 9: Steamy Hot Intimate Scene (Olivia's POV)

After several days of tension and emotional push-pull, Olivia confronts Kaden about his sudden withdrawal. The conversation escalates into a heated moment where their passions collide once more. They find themselves caught up in an electric embrace, yielding to their desires. Their chemistry ignites as they share a passionate night together filled with discovery and vulnerability, breaking down the walls both had built.

Chapter 10: Internal Falling in Love (Kaden's POV)

In the aftermath of their intimate encounter, Kaden wakes up feeling a mix of exhilaration and clarity. He realizes he's unable to ignore his feelings for Olivia any longer; he's truly in love with her. As they share quiet moments during the day, he finds himself falling deeper into the overwhelming joy she brings him. Kaden begins to visualize a future that includes Olivia, but worry still gnaws at him about how to balance their two lives.

Chapter 11: Dark Moment/Pulling Apart (Olivia's POV)

Just as things seem to be going perfectly, a misunderstanding occurs when Kaden's tech company announces a major project that requires him to leave town for an extended period. Olivia misinterprets Kaden's excitement as a sign that he's ready to move on, pushing her to retreat into her own fears of being abandoned again. This dark moment leads to a painful conversation where wounds from their past resurface, leaving them both feeling vulnerable and uncertain about the strength of their bond.

Chapter 12: Resolution (Kaden's POV)

Kaden, devastated by their separation, realizes he cannot let their differences and misunderstandings dictate their future. He goes to Olivia, baring his soul and explaining how deeply he has come to care for her, emphasizing that love is about supporting each other's dreams. Kaden encourages Olivia to embrace her art, and he reveals his intention to balance his commitments while cherishing their relationship. They both agree to work through their fears together, solidifying their partnership.

Epilogue: HEA (Olivia's POV)

Several months later, Olivia stands in her own art gallery, surrounded by friends and family at her opening night. Kaden is by her side, proudly supporting her dream. Their relationship blossoms as they continue to blend their lives, creating beautiful memories together. As Olivia gives a heartfelt speech, she glances at Kaden and realizes that true love flourishes when we show our scars and celebrate each other's growth. In that moment, she knows they have created a love that can withstand any challenges life throws their way.

Outline for Campus Love Story

Chapter 1: Intro to Heroine (Stacy)

- Stacy's Perspective: Introduced as the quintessential sorority queen, Stacy Harper is portrayed as confident and fiercely ambitious. Despite her bubbly exterior, she struggles with the pressure to maintain her reputation and meet her high-achieving family's expectations, revealing glimpses of her vulnerability under the surface.

Chapter 2: Intro to Hero (Bryce)

- Bryce's Perspective: Bryce Thompson is the charismatic star of the college basketball team, hailed as a hero on campus. He revels in the attention but secretly fears that people love him only for his athletic prowess. He dreams of pursuing a career in sports management, hoping to be recognized for his abilities off the court.

Chapter 3: Meet Cute

- Stacy's Perspective: In the bustling cafeteria, Stacy spills her drink on Bryce while arguing with her friends about his recent game performance. Their heated exchange sets the tone for their contentious relationship, as she rolls her eyes at his jock persona and he smirks back, clearly unfazed.

Chapter 4: Growing Attraction/Getting to Know Each Other

- Bryce's Perspective: During the snowstorm, which leads them into the library, Bryce reflects on Stacy's fierce personality and hidden depths. He discovers she's not just a superficial sorority girl but has real ambition and talents as an artist, sparking curiosity in him to learn more.

Chapter 5: First Kiss

- Stacy's Perspective: As they spend more time together in the library, their banter becomes more playful, and Stacy feels an undeniable spark. During a moment of laughter, they lean in unexpectedly, sharing a tentative first kiss that leaves them both breathless and confused about what is happening between them.

Chapter 6: Her Smell

- Bryce's Perspective: Bryce becomes increasingly aware of Stacy's captivating scent—a mix of floral and citrus that enchants him. This scent lingers on his clothes and fills his thoughts, igniting fascination and stirring emotions he never expected as they interact more outside of the library.

Chapter 7: His Taste

- Stacy's Perspective: After they share a celebratory hot cocoa on a snowy evening, Stacy savors the unique taste of Bryce's laughter, feeling exhilarated by his warmth. Between playful teasing and heartfelt moments, she realizes how much she enjoys being with him despite their differences.

Chapter 8: Internal Conflict/Resistance to Attraction

- Bryce's Perspective: Bryce grapples with feelings of attraction towards Stacy, struggling to reconcile his burgeoning feelings with the stereotypes he's always had about sorority girls. He fears that if he lets his guard down, he might lose himself in a relationship that feels too complicated.

Chapter 9: Steamy Hot Intimate Scene

- Stacy's Perspective: One night, after a group study session that turns into a more intimate gathering, Stacy and Bryce find themselves alone again. Their chemistry ignites, and they share a passionate kiss that leads to a steamy encounter, pushing boundaries and leaving them both exhilarated yet confused.

Chapter 10: Internal Falling in Love

- Bryce's Perspective: As weeks pass, Bryce's feelings deepen for Stacy. He realizes that she challenges him, inspires him, and complements him in ways he never thought possible. Love begins to blossom, but he struggles with how their friends and families will react to their relationship.

Chapter 11: Dark Moment/Pulling Apart

- Stacy's Perspective: Rumors begin to swirl on campus about their relationship, leading Stacy to question if Bryce truly sees her as more than just a sorority sister. A confrontation following a public incident makes them both retreat into their insecurities, and an emotional fallout leaves them heartbroken and distanced.

Chapter 12: Resolution

- Bryce's Perspective: After some self-reflection, Bryce realizes that his feelings for Stacy are genuine and worth fighting for. He publicly stands up for her amidst the gossip and confronts the misconceptions they both faced. His heartfelt declaration helps to mend their relationship, allowing them to find common ground and communicate openly about their fears.

Epilogue: Happy Ever After (HEA)

- Stacy and Bryce, Dual Perspective: Several months later, Stacy and Bryce thrive in their relationship as they balance basketball games and art exhibits, having forged a path that celebrates their individuality. They attend a winter formal together, confident in their love and excited for the future, embodying the idea that love can grow from the most unexpected circumstances. Their union inspires others on campus, proving that true connection transcends social stereotypes.

Title: Rodeo Rivalry

Chapter 1: Maddie's POV - Intro to Heroine

Maddie Blake is at the top of her game as a barrel racer, training hard for the upcoming rodeo season. She's fiercely independent and has dedicated her life to her sport after years of sweeping victories. She reflects on the sacrifices she's made and how her hard work has shaped her identity, but there's a nagging loneliness beneath her success. Despite her accolades, she feels vulnerable as new competitors emerge.

Chapter 2: Sierra's POV - Intro to Hero

Sierra Lawson is an exuberant and ambitious newcomer, fresh out of high school and ready to prove herself in the rodeo circuit. She's cocky, confident, and untested—but brimming with raw talent that she believes might just shake up the industry. Sierra's family ties to rodeo spur her determination to rise to the top and earn the respect of veterans like Maddie. She dreams of becoming a legend in her own right.

Chapter 3: Meet Cute (Maddie's POV)

Maddie first encounters Sierra at a press event, where reporters are buzzing about the rookie's meteoric rise and potential. When Sierra makes the offhand comment about whether racing Maddie would even be 'a race,' Maddie feels her blood boil. Livid, she approaches the sassy newcomer to confront her, leading to an electric exchange filled with tension and sarcasm.

Chapter 4: Growing Attraction/Getting to Know Each Other (Sierra's POV)

As weeks pass and the rodeo circuit heats up, Sierra finds herself drawn to Maddie's fierce tenacity and impressive skills. While she's initially focused on competition, she starts to admire Maddie's dedication and strength. During a training session, she tries to pick Maddie's brain, sensing an unexpected connection building beneath their rivalry.

Chapter 5: First Kiss (Maddie's POV)

During a late-night practice session, Maddie and Sierra find themselves alone after a grueling day of training. They get caught in a heated argument filled with tension that spins into a spontaneous moment. Emboldened by frustration and a spark of electricity, Maddie grabs Sierra and kisses her. It's passionate and overwhelming, leaving both of them stunned and breathless afterward.

Chapter 6: Her Smell (Sierra's POV)

As Sierra reflects on the kiss, she can't stop thinking about Maddie and the intoxicating scent of leather and horses that lingers on her skin. Sierra reminisces about Maddie's beauty, her steely determination, and the way she feels alive whenever they're near. Chatting with her best friend, Sierra finds herself blushing as she admits to developing feelings for the very woman she initially set out to beat.

Chapter 7: His Taste (Maddie's POV)

Maddie, too, is consumed by their kiss. Alone in her trailer, she confides in a longtime rodeo friend about the unexpected swirl of emotions she feels regarding Sierra. Maddie tastes the lingering sensation on her lips even though it leaves her confused. Was it just a moment of heated rivalry, or is there something deeper brewing beneath the surface?

Chapter 8: Internal Conflict/Resistance to Attraction (Sierra's POV)

Despite her attraction, Sierra wrestles with her feelings for Maddie. The fear of being known as just a rebellious newcomer often leads her to bristle against her own emotions. She wants to win the title but grapples with the realization that pursuing her feelings for Maddie may jeopardize her chances at success. Doubt creates distance between them.

Chapter 9: Steamy Hot Intimate Scene (Maddie's POV)

One evening after an exhausting rodeo, Maddie and Sierra retreat to Maddie's trailer to celebrate. Laughter turns to flirtation, and suddenly, they're enveloped in a passionate embrace that spills over into a steamy night of intimacy. Their connection deepens as they explore each other's bodies and vulnerabilities, shattering the barriers of rivalry between them.

Chapter 10: Internal Falling in Love (Sierra's POV)

After their steamy night, Sierra realizes she has fallen hard for Maddie. She's challenged by her own stubbornness and pride as they continue to train together in preparation for the next competition. The thrill of her races starts to pale in comparison to the joy Maddie brings her. Sierra begins to envision a future where she can celebrate both her competitive spirit and her connection to Maddie.

Chapter 11: Dark Moment/Pulling Apart (Maddie's POV)

As the rodeo event approaches, tensions rise. Maddie overhears Sierra discussing her dreams of winning and how she plans to take

Maddie down. Feeling betrayed, Maddie confronts Sierra in a heated argument, fueled by jealousy and fear. In the heat of the moment, they separate, leaving both women feeling lost and heartbroken, unsure if they can ever truly reconcile their rivalry and their feelings.

Chapter 12: Resolution (Sierra's POV)

As the final competition draws near, both women realize how much they mean to one another. In a moment of clarity, Sierra decides to seek Maddie out and apologize sincerely, vowing to embrace the connection they've built rather than let old rivalry consume them. After heartfelt discussions and shared vulnerability, they decide to race together, not as enemies, but as partners in competition and love.

Epilogue: HEA (Maddie's POV)

In the aftermath of the rodeo, Maddie and Sierra stand together, celebrating their achievements and the powerful bond they've forged. They've become icons not only on the circuit but also for those who dare to love beyond rivalry. Their future looks promising as they plan joint events, intertwine their lives, and revel in their deepening love together, prepared to face the road ahead as a united front.

Outline for Adrenaline Hearts

Chapter 1: Intro to Heroine (Lila's POV)

Lila Grant, a meticulous high school teacher and nature enthusiast, finds her comfort zone in planning and organization. While she has a love for the outdoors, she prefers peaceful hikes and quaint picnics to death-defying adventures. As she gears up to join a rafting trip at the insistence of her thrill-seeking friends, Lila reflects on her frustrations, feeling pulled between her friends' adventurous spirit and her desire for a more settled life.

Chapter 2: Intro to Hero (Chase's POV)

Chase Carpenter is a well-known social media influencer thriving on the thrills of extreme sports. Living life on the edge, he relishes each exhilarating moment and is perpetually on the hunt for his next wild adventure. As he gears up for the same rafting trip, he revels in his upcoming social media post, confident that it will turbocharge his already growing fame. Amidst the excitement, he brushes off any thoughts of responsibility, convincing himself that he is invincible.

Chapter 3: Meet Cute (Lila's POV)

During the rafting trip's chaotic launch, Lila awkwardly stumbles into Chase, completely soaked as she grapples with her raft. Their initial encounter is peppered with irritation and miscommunication; Chase's goofy confidence annoys Lila, while Lila's cautious demeanor frustrates Chase. The exchange sets the stage for a rivalry to develop, leaving both of them determined to prove their contrasting views correct.

Chapter 4: Growing Attraction/Getting to Know Each Other (Chase's POV)

Despite their rocky start, Chase can't shake off Lila from his mind. While navigating the river, he observes her tenacity and unexpected bravery when faced with challenges. He notices how she encourages others when they struggle, earning his respect. Through lighthearted banter, he starts to unravel layers of her personality that he finds captivating, and he feels the thrill of unexpected attraction slowly creeping in.

Chapter 5: First Kiss (Lila's POV)

After a particularly chaotic yet thrilling day on the river, the group sets up camp. As Chase and Lila share stories over a campfire, their playful teasing escalates into passionate banter. An inciting moment occurs when Chase reaches over to brush a stray hair from Lila's face. Their eyes lock, and in a moment of spontaneity, Lila leans forward and kisses him, igniting sparks between them. Both are left breathless and reeling from the intensity of the unexpected moment.

Chapter 6: Her Smell (Chase's POV)

In the aftermath of the kiss, Chase begins to notice the aromas that come to define Lila: fresh lavender from her shampoo mixed with the crisp scent of pine from the forest. He can't help but be distracted by the memory of her soft lips against his. A fellow adventurer comments on Chase's change in demeanor, teasing him about his infatuation, prompting Chase to deflect but secretly revel in the acknowledgment of his feelings for Lila.

Chapter 7: His Taste (Lila's POV)

Later, while confiding in her friend after a long day, Lila reflects on the kiss. She recalls the sweetness of Chase's lips, the thrill it sparked in her chest, and how it felt so right despite their differences. She feels an intoxicating blend of excitement and dread, knowing they come from two different worlds. She's hesitant to embrace her feelings, fearing exposure to the thrill of a relationship could change everything.

Chapter 8: Internal Conflict/Resistance to Attraction (Chase's POV)

As their chemistry grows stronger, Chase grapples with his own conflicts. Torn between his free-spirited nature and a growing attachment to Lila, he worries that pursuing her could mean sacrificing his lifestyle or putting her in dangerous situations. He convinces himself that their differing desires could never mesh, leading him to take a step back from their newfound connection, all while desperately wishing to be by her side.

Chapter 9: Steamy Hot Intimate Scene (Lila's POV)

One moonlit night during a break in their adventure, Lila and Chase find themselves alone by the campfire. The intensity of their feelings erupts into a passionate kiss that quickly escalates into a steamy encounter beneath the stars. Caught up in the moment, they explore each other with fervor, breaking down the walls they had built. In this intimate embrace, they discover a deeper connection that ignites their senses.

Chapter 10: Internal Falling in Love (Chase's POV)

In the days following their passionate night, Chase realizes he is falling in love with Lila. Every moment spent together—from laughter to shared adventures—deepens his affection for her. He admires how she embraces challenges, showcasing her spirit and heart. He begins to envision a future that combines their thrilling lives, leaving him yearning to understand how he can mesh both worlds together.

Chapter 11: Dark Moment/Pulling Apart (Lila's POV)

When the trip is nearing its end, Lila learns about Chase's plans to travel for his next extreme sports challenge, which threatens to separate them. Conflicted, she questions whether their relationship can withstand the distance. During a heated discussion after a misunderstood comment of Chase's about her safety obsession, Lila retreats. She feels their connection slip away as Chase's carefree spirit clashes with her longing for stability.

Chapter 12: Resolution (Chase's POV)

Determined to win back Lila, Chase reflects on the journey they shared and realizes that love isn't about reckless abandon; it's about embracing each togetherness and supporting their dreams. He tracks down Lila, laying all his feelings bare, assuring her that he can compromise and that he values her balance in his life. With newfound clarity, they come to an understanding that allows them both to pursue their passions while cherishing their relationship.

Epilogue: HEA (Lila's POV)

Months later, Lila and Chase find themselves on a new adventure—hiking to a breathtaking viewpoint. Both have integrated their worlds; Lila embraces her adventurous side, while Chase learns the beauty of slowing down and being present. As they look over the stunning landscape, Lila takes Chase's hand, grateful for the thrilling journey that brought them together. They exchange a knowing smile, hearts intertwined, ready to conquer every adventure—together.

Title: Love and Familial Ties

Chapter 1: Intro to Heroine (Sophia)

- Sophia's Perspective: Introduced as a strong-willed young woman, Sophia Rossini feels trapped by her affluent but controlling family, who imposes high expectations for her life. Sophia dreams of traveling and seeking adventure, feeling suffocated by the impending obligation of an arranged marriage for strategic family alliances.

Chapter 2: Intro to Hero (Cash)

- Cash's Perspective: Cash Ferrari is introduced as an heir to a powerful mafia family, raised in the shadows of organized crime. He is ambitious and dreams of moving beyond the criminal world, but feels the immense pressure from his father to conform to traditional family ideals. The weight of legacy looms over him as he faces the obligation to marry to solidify family power.

Chapter 3: Meet Cute

- Sophia's Perspective: On the day of the wedding, elegance and tension fill the air at the ancient cathedral. As Sophia stands at the altar, she catches a glimpse of Cash, who looks equally apprehensive. Their eyes meet in a moment of shared uncertainty, and despite the circumstances, an electric spark ignites.

Chapter 4: Growing Attraction/Getting to Know Each Other

- Cash's Perspective: After the shocking wedding ceremony, Cash and Sophia leave together, still processing their unexpected fates. As they navigate the chaos of their new roles, they begin to share their personal stories, revealing their aspirations and fears, and the chemistry develops beneath the surface.

Chapter 5: First Kiss

- Sophia's Perspective: One evening, as they share a quiet moment escaping the noise of their families, Cash steps closer, hesitating before leaning in. Their first kiss is tentative at first, filled with uncertainty but quickly becomes passionate as they both feel the undeniable connection.

Chapter 6: His Taste

- Sophia's Perspective: After a romantic dinner, Sophia gets lost in the taste of Cash's laughter and the warmth of his presence. Their playful banter turns flirty, leaving her enamored. She realizes that despite their forced circumstances, there's something genuine stirring between them.

Chapter 7: Her Smell

- Cash's Perspective: Discovering Sophia's intoxicating scent—a mix of vanilla and a hint of tempting citrus—Cash finds himself drawn to her even more. It lingers in his mind, a comforting reminder of their budding relationship, contrasting with the chaos of mafia life swirling around them.

Chapter 8: Internal Conflict/Resistance to Attraction

- Cash's Perspective: Cash battles with his growing feelings for Sophia, feeling guilty for wanting her in a world filled with betrayal and danger. He struggles with loyalty to his family's legacy while reconciling that she represents the change he desperately seeks.

Chapter 9: Steamy Hot Intimate Scene

- Sophia's Perspective: During a particularly heated moment after a family event, their shared frustrations boil over. In the safety of their home, they succumb to the passion that has built between them, leading to an intimate night. It's both exhilarating and terrifying, signifying a shift in their relationship.

Chapter 10: Internal Falling in Love

- Cash's Perspective: Cash starts to recognize the love growing between them, realizing he wants more than just a marriage of convenience. He dreams of a future together, one that could redefine his family's legacy and remove them from the shadow of organized crime.

Chapter 11: Dark Moment/Pulling Apart

- Sophia's Perspective: Just as things seem to be falling into place, an unexpected betrayal from within the family surfaces, putting them at risk. Sophia receives threatening messages that suggest their union is seen as a weakness within the mafia circles, leading her to pull away from Cash in fear for her safety.

Chapter 12: Resolution

- Cash's Perspective: Cash confronts the betrayal head-on, realizing he must fight for both his love for Sophia and their newfound dreams of legitimacy. He creates a plan to counter the threats and secure their future, showing Sophia that love and loyalty can coexist even in a world of shadows.

Epilogue: Happy Ever After (HEA)

- Sophia and Cash, Dual Perspective: A year later, Sophia and Cash navigate their lives as partners—not only in marriage but also in reforming the family business toward legitimacy. They've faced down rival families and internal strife, emerging stronger and more united. Their love has transformed their families' legacy, and they look forward to a future built on trust, love, and ambition, free from the chains of their past.

Outline for Squirrel

Chapter 1: Intro to Heroine (Lisa's POV)

Lisa Brooks, now a successful graphic designer in her late twenties, reflects on her childhood in Riverbend. Over coffee in a quaint café, she remembers the happy chaos of her youth, especially moments spent with Mason, the boy next door who playfully teased her and somehow became a part of her identity. Although she has moved on and built a new life, memories of her childhood crush linger, intertwined with feelings of frustration over the nickname Squirrel because she couldn't quite pronounce the r's in the word.

Chapter 2: Intro to Hero (Mason's POV)

Mason Hayes, now a charismatic entrepreneur, stands in his spacious backyard, looking through old photos. He recalls the innocent mischief of his childhood, including his playful nickname for Lisa, which he used to hide his feelings. Mason narrates his journey from a playful boy to a successful man, but beneath his confident exterior lies a nostalgia for the simplicity of those earlier days and a longing for Lisa.

Chapter 3: Meet Cute (Lisa's POV)

Lisa returns home to Riverbend to help her mother organize the community fair. While in the market, she unexpectedly bumps into Mason, stirring old feelings and confounding her with his charm. Their banter picks up right where they left off, filled with old jokes, and teasing. Mason's playful insistence on her nickname instantly annoys her, reigniting both their youthful rivalry and buried attraction.

Chapter 4: Growing Attraction/Getting to Know Each Other (Mason's POV)

Mason finds himself drawn to Lisa's confident demeanor and stunning creativity, watching her interact with townsfolk as if she were right at home. Their time together is filled with shared laughter over childhood memories, remembrances of their antics, and familiar tensions that bring them closer. The more they interact, the more Mason notices Lisa's stunning smile and grace, igniting sparks that he can't ignore.

Chapter 5: First Kiss (Lisa's POV)

After a long day of setting up for the fair, Lisa and Mason find themselves alone in the now-familiar oak tree near their childhood homes. The air is thick with tension as they reminisce and playfully argue. In a moment of emotional spontaneity, Lisa impulsively kisses Mason, overwhelmed by a flood of feelings. The kiss surprises them both, deepening their connection and leaving Lisa breathless and questioning.

Chapter 6: Her Smell (Mason's POV)

As Mason reflects on that incredible kiss, he can't shake the enchanting scent of Lisa—a blend of lavender and fresh-baked cookies. The memory comes to life every time he sees her, rekindling flames of attraction. A friend notices his preoccupation and playfully accuses him of being head over heels for Squirrel. Mason tries to brush it off, but internally, he knows he's falling hard.

Chapter 7: His Taste (Lisa's POV)

Later that night, Lisa lies in bed replaying their kiss, indulging in the softness of it and Mason's warmth. Confiding in her best friend over video call, she admits she felt electricity and hope but also fears of what pursuing a relationship could mean. The thrill of that kiss both excites and terrifies her—could Mason really be more than just a childhood friend?

Chapter 8: Internal Conflict/Resistance to Attraction (Mason's POV)

Despite his feelings, Mason wrestles with the fear that their past could complicate a potential relationship. Whenever he sees Lisa, the shared memories clash with the worry that he could lose her again if things don't work out. He becomes distant, trying to behave as if everything is normal while struggling internally with his feelings and decisions.

Chapter 9: Steamy Hot Intimate Scene (Lisa's POV)

During the town's fair, the chemistry reaches a boiling point under the colorful night sky. After a heartfelt moment during the festivities, Lisa and Mason can no longer contain their desire. They sneak away to the community theater, where passion consumes them. Their intimate encounter is a mix of urgency and tenderness, sealing the thin line between friendship and romance.

Chapter 10: Internal Falling in Love (Mason's POV)

As days pass, Mason becomes painfully aware of how deeply he's fallen for Lisa. He admires her strength, wit, and artistic spirit, feeling utterly captivated every time she flashes that sunny smile. He worries that he's let his fear of commitment push her away. Mason starts to consider a future with Lisa, thinking of what a life together could look like.

Chapter 11: Dark Moment/Pulling Apart (Lisa's POV)

Just as they begin to explore their feelings openly, a misunderstanding occurs at the fair, causing a rift. Mason reacts impulsively out of embarrassment, making a flippant comment that hurts Lisa deeply. Feeling abandoned again, Lisa retreats, convinced that their childhood dynamic is repeating and that love is just a fleeting dream. Their once joyful connection becomes clouded by pain as they both withdraw.

Chapter 12: Resolution (Mason's POV)

Realizing how much he values Lisa's presence in his life, Mason makes a heartfelt effort to apologize. He surprises her on the final night of the fair, pouring out his feelings and how he views their relationship with clarity. He refuses to let past fears dictate his future. Lisa, touched by his sincerity, recognizes the love that blossomed between them. They reconcile, laughing over old nicknames and reaffirming their bond, ready to embrace what lies ahead.

Epilogue: HEA (Lisa's POV)

Months later, Lisa and Mason find joy in their relationship, navigating life as true partners—balancing work and love while appreciating their shared past. At a local art showcase, where Lisa reveals her latest installation themed around their childhood, she feels grateful for her journey. With a playful smile, Mason leans in and affectionately whispers Squirrel, making her heart flutter. As they embrace, Lisa knows they've transformed their childhood rivalry into an enduring love story, ready to face whatever comes next together.

Bonus: 10 prompts: Age Gap, Sports Romance & Western

Title: Numbers and Love on the Range

Chapter 1: Felicity's POV - Intro to Heroine

Felicity Collins is an overworked accountant in a bustling city, drowning in spreadsheets and deadlines. She reflects on her lack of a love life and the burnt-out feeling that has come to define her existence. A recent nerve-wracking day at work pushes her to finally accept her friends' invitation to escape to a dude ranch.

Chapter 2: Hank's POV - Intro to Hero

Hank Harrison is introduced as the rugged owner of a struggling dude ranch, balancing the demands of running his family's legacy with the reality of financial decline. He works hard but feels isolated, unsure if he can save his dream and the ranch's future. His thoughts reveal a quiet determination mixed with fear of failure.

Chapter 3: Meet Cute (Felicity's POV)

Felicity arrives at the ranch, feeling slightly out of her element in her city clothes. During a chaotic welcome dinner, she accidentally runs into Hank while attempting to carry a bucket of feed. They share an awkward but amusing exchange that sets the stage for their initial chemistry, leaving them both flustered.

Chapter 4: Growing Attraction/Getting to Know Each Other (Hank's POV)

As the days pass, Felicity and Hank find themselves working together more often. Hank admires Felicity's organizational skills as she jumps in to help with the ranch finances. They have playful banter and throaty laughs while sorting through receipts, growing comfortable with each other. Hank starts to see Felicity not just as a city gal but someone capable and intriguing.

Chapter 5: First Kiss (Felicity's POV)

After a long day of work, Hank and Felicity share a moment on the porch, watching the sunset spill colors across the sky. Overwhelmed by their growing connection, they lean in for their first kiss, a tentative yet passionate moment that leaves them both breathless.

Chapter 6: Her Smell (Hank's POV)

Now unable to focus on his duties without being distracted by Felicity, Hank finds himself thinking about her scent—fresh and floral, like a gentle summer breeze. He's reminded of her beauty and kindness whenever they share brief encounters. His ranch hand, Ryan, teases him about his obvious crush on a "city girl," further reminding Hank of his feelings.

Chapter 7: His Taste (Felicity's POV)

Alone in her room after their kiss, Felicity can't shake off the electricity that sparked between them. She reflects on the moment and remembers the taste of Hank's lips and the warmth of his arms around her. Giddy and hopeful, she confesses to her friends how irresistible Hank has become.

Chapter 8: Internal Conflict/Resistance to Attraction (Hank's POV)

Despite their chemistry, Hank wrestles with his feelings. He questions if pursuing something serious with Felicity is wise, considering the ranch's financial troubles. He fears that if he opens his heart, he might lose everything—his dreams, his livelihood, and potentially, Felicity.

Chapter 9: Steamy Hot Intimate Scene (Felicity's POV)

In a moment of raw passion ignited by a heated argument about the ranch, Hank and Felicity give in to their desires. They share a steamy night together in the cozy cabin, feeling liberated within their embrace amid the uncertainty that looms over the ranch.

Chapter 10: Internal Falling in Love (Hank's POV)

While spending more time with Felicity, Hank starts envisioning a life with her. He realizes he's falling in love with her but feels torn between his responsibilities and his heart. He wrestles with self-doubt and the fear that he might not be able to provide for her.

Chapter 11: Dark Moment/Pulling Apart (Felicity's POV)

The following morning, Felicity sees a bank notice on the ranch bulletin board about a foreclosure risk. Feeling cornered by Hank's struggles and uncertain if she should stay to help or protect her own heart, she pulls away, deciding to leave the ranch early to reflect on her priorities.

Chapter 12: Resolution (Hank's POV)

In the aftermath of Felicity's departure, Hank understands he needs to confront not only his financial issues head-on but also his feelings. He takes decisive steps to save the ranch, realizing that love is worth fighting for. He rushes to the city to find Felicity and explain everything.

Epilogue: HEA (Felicity's POV)

Months later, Felicity returns to the ranch—not just as a visitor, but ready to invest in it both personally and professionally. With Hank embracing the accounting support she provides, they find a balance between work and love. Together, they turn the ranch around and create a beautiful life, facing every challenge side by side, solidifying their happily ever after.

Outline for Cheer for Love

Chapter 1: Intro to Heroine (Holly's POV)

Holly Carter juggles her roles as an NFL cheerleader and part-time college student, showcasing her dedication to fitness and performance. Behind her beaming smile, Holly struggles with the misconceptions surrounding her job, highlighting the harsh realities of objectification and disrespect that cheerleaders often face. As she prepares for a high-stakes game, she reflects on her dreams of being respected as an athlete and a professional, and her longing for real connection.

Chapter 2: Intro to Hero (Jaxon's POV)

Jaxon Mitchell, the rookie quarterback for the home team, is introduced during a tense practice session. He's determined to prove himself on the field, especially after being drafted into the NFL amid high expectations. As he navigates the pressures of being a professional athlete, Jaxon has a strong sense of morality and respect for women, shaped by his upbringing. He views cheerleaders as valuable members of the team but knows that dating one could complicate his position in the league.

Chapter 3: Meet Cute (Holly's POV)

During a high-energy halftime performance, Holly becomes the target of a boisterous fan who throws a hot dog at her. Just as she's about to lose her cool and abandon the routine, Jaxon rushes in to defend her and confronts the fan, causing a scene. After the game, Holly finds herself unexpectedly drawn to Jaxon when he approaches her to apologize for the fan's behavior and introduces himself, marking the start of their connection.

Chapter 4: Growing Attraction/Getting to Know Each Other (Jaxon's POV)

Over the next few weeks, Holly and Jaxon exchange texts and gradually decide to meet outside of game day. They bond over shared experiences and find solace in each other's company. Jaxon learns more about the challenges Holly faces as a cheerleader, gaining a newfound respect for her dedication. Holly is captivated by Jaxon's charming personality and genuine nature beneath the quarterback facade, deepening their chemistry with each encounter.

Chapter 5: First Kiss (Holly's POV)

After a fun dinner and a shared laugh at a local diner, Holly and Jaxon share a nervous glance as they linger outside her apartment. The attraction that has been building culminates in a passionate first kiss that sends electricity tingling through their bodies. Holly, feeling overwhelmed and exhilarated, realizes she never wants to pull away, capturing the essence of their growing relationship. The moment leaves both breathless yet aware of what is at stake.

Chapter 6: Her Smell (Jaxon's POV)

As Jaxon reflects on their kiss, he can't help but think of the intoxicating scent of Holly—freshly washed hair mixed with sweat and a hint of floral perfume. He recalls how her laughter brightened the dimly lit space of the diner, her beauty juxtaposed against the chaos of their lives. Unable to resist, he confides his feelings about Holly to his close friend and teammate, who teases him about his undeniable crush on the cheerleader, prompting Jaxon to realize how strongly he feels for her.

Chapter 7: His Taste (Holly's POV)

In her apartment after their date, Holly can still taste the warmth of Jaxon's lips while thinking about their first kiss. Confiding in her roommate, she explains how exhilarating it was, contrasting with her apprehension about dating within the NFL's strict guidelines. Although thrilled by the kiss, she worries about the potential fallout if it is discovered. The lingering heat of their connection leaves her dreaming of a future with him, yet she battles her internal fears.

Chapter 8: Internal Conflict/Resistance to Attraction (Jaxon's POV)

As their relationship deepens, Jaxon finds himself torn between his growing feelings for Holly and the pressures of NFL culture. He grapples with the 'unwritten rule' about dating cheerleaders and what it might mean for his career, causing him to pull back and keep a distance he doesn't want. Jaxon's internal struggle weighs heavy as he feels guilty for wanting to pursue a relationship that could attract unwanted attention and jeopardize his ambitions.

Chapter 9: Steamy Hot Intimate Scene (Holly's POV)

During a secret rendezvous at Jaxon's apartment after a late practice, the air is thick with tension. As they talk about their childhood aspirations and dreams, the conversation soon ignites into a passionate and heated encounter that culminates in a night of intimacy unlike any Holly has experienced before. They explore each other's hearts while losing themselves physically, deepening their bond and sense of intimacy in a place where they feel safe.

Chapter 10: Internal Falling in Love (Jaxon's POV)

In the days following their steamy night, Jaxon starts to see not only Holly's beauty but also her strength and resilience. He falls deeper for her, viewing her as an equal who challenges him to be a better man. He relishes the small moments they share—the laughter, the connection, the understanding between them. Jaxon realizes that being with Holly brings out the best in him, and he wants to support her fight for respect within the football community.

Chapter 11: Dark Moment/Pulling Apart (Holly's POV)

After a game where the media speculates on Holly and Jaxon's relationship, the pressure becomes unbearable, leading to a confrontation between them. Holly feels caught in the crossfire of fans trailing her and rumors about "cheerleader distractions." Hurt by Jaxon's hesitation to go public with their relationship, she feels resentment simmering beneath the surface. In a moment of anger, she tells him they should not see each other anymore, breaking both their hearts.

Chapter 12: Resolution (Jaxon's POV)

Driven by determination, Jaxon confronts the media storm that's taken over their lives. He defends Holly publicly, choosing to expose the unfair treatment and objectification of cheerleaders while voicing his admiration for Holly's strength. Realizing how much she means to him, Jaxon reaches out to Holly, professing his love and commitment to fighting for change together. They reconnect, vowing to stand united against the cultural norms that threaten to tear them apart.

Epilogue with HEA (Holly's & Jaxon's POV)

Months later, Holly and Jaxon stand hand in hand at a charity event focused on empowering cheerleaders and promoting respect within sports. The atmosphere is electric as Holly takes the stage to address the crowd, flanked by Jaxon, who beams with pride. Together, they reflect on their journey—dealing with the challenges and ultimately embracing love amidst the chaos. With newfound respect and understanding, they celebrate their relationship and the impact they're making, ready to face the future, together.

Title: Cowboy Life

Chapter 1: Intro to Heroine - Jane's POV

Jane Mitchell is introduced as a bustling urbanite navigating her life in the city. She dreams of adventure and has a love for storytelling, but when it comes to reality, she feels bound by her mundane routine, realizing that's why she ultimately broke things off with her well-meaning yet predictable fiancé, Brad. She reflects on her life choices, recognizing her longing for something more but feeling trapped by societal expectations and her own fears of stepping outside her comfort zone.

Chapter 2: Intro to Hero - Cooper's POV

Cooper Hayes enters the scene as a ruggedly handsome ranch hand. We glimpse his life on the ranch, where he finds joy in the simplicity of nature and the camaraderie of fellow ranchers. However, Cooper wrestles with the weight of family responsibilities and his desire for adventure beyond the ranch. He's confident and competent, revealing both his charming wit and the depth of his character as he dreams of exploring the world beyond the ranch while also hoping to find someone who truly sees him.

Chapter 3: Meet Cute - Jane's POV

Upon arriving at Cooper's family ranch for her lessons, Jane is a whirlwind of nerves. When she meets Cooper, she awkwardly stumbles over her words and trips on her own feet, showcasing her lack of ranch skills right from the start. Cooper's warm smile and easy laugh instantly put her at ease and sparks an unintentional chemistry between them that neither can ignore.

Chapter 4: Growing Attraction/Getting to Know Each Other - Cooper's POV

As Jane begins her lessons, the growing attraction between her and Cooper deepens in this chapter. They engage in playful banter as she gradually learns the ropes of ranch life, and he showcases his rugged expertise. Each interaction reveals more of their personalities: Jane's witty humor contrasts with Cooper's laid-back confidence. In their conversations, they share stories about their lives, backgrounds, and dreams, slowly breaking down the walls around their hearts.

Chapter 5: First Kiss - Jane's POV

During a sunset lesson after a successful horseback ride through the stunning trails, the tension reaches a breaking point. Surrounded by the breathtaking landscape, Jane and Cooper find themselves in a moment where unspoken feelings surface. Their eyes lock, and the world fades away as they lean in for their first kiss—warm and passionate, filled with all the emotions they've been holding back. Jane is shocked yet exhilarated by the intensity of their connection.

Chapter 6: Her Smell - Cooper's POV

After their first kiss, Cooper can't shake Jane's lingering scent—a sweet floral aroma mixed with sunshine that captures his senses. As he reflects on their kiss, he is constantly reminded of her beauty and charm, and he feels an intense longing for her. His friends on the ranch notice his distracted demeanor, teasing him about the "city girl" who's stolen his heart, making Cooper both flustered and amused by their insights into his feelings for Jane.

Chapter 7: His Taste - Jane's POV

In the aftermath of their kiss, Jane lies awake in bed, replaying the moment in her mind. As she recalls the taste of Cooper's lips, a mixture of warmth and genuine affection, she confides her thoughts to her sister over a video call. Torn between excitement and fear, Jane grapples with her feelings for Cooper and her commitment to Brad, realizing that this unexpected connection may change everything.

Chapter 8: Internal Conflict/Resistance to Attraction - Cooper's POV

Faced with growing feelings, Cooper is conflicted. While he's falling for Jane, he worries about her serious relationship with Brad and whether she's ready to embrace a life on the ranch. Torn between pursuing his emotions and respecting her commitment, he puts distance between them, attempting to focus on teaching her the skills she needs while silently longing for her.

Chapter 9: Steamy Hot Intimate Scene - Jane's POV

After a particularly exhausting day of gathering and sorting cattle for the upcoming fair, Jane and Cooper find themselves alone in the barn. The sparks fly, and the tension escalates into a heated, passionate encounter, where they share more than just a kiss—filled with deep longing and unspoken desires. Jane feels liberated while also conflicted and guilty about how easily she loses herself in Cooper's embrace.

Chapter 10: Internal Falling in Love - Cooper's POV

As the days pass and their secret moments together accumulate, Cooper realizes he's fallen for Jane in ways he never anticipated. He admires her courage to step out of her city girl comfort zone and appreciates the strength she brings to his life. He envisions a future where they run the ranch together, but his fears of losing her unfairly weigh heavily on his heart, knowing her ties to Brad.

Chapter 11: Dark Moment/Pulling Apart - Jane's POV

The joyous moments come crashing down when Jane receives a surprise visit from Brad. He expresses his excitement about the possibility of reigniting their engagement and the upcoming wedding and the life they had planned, forcing Jane to confront her feelings. Conflicted and overwhelmed, she pushes Cooper away and contemplates returning home to her old life. Hurt and heartbroken, Cooper tries to respect her decision but feels lost without her.

Chapter 12: Resolution - Cooper's POV

Cooper decides to confront Jane before she makes any final decisions. In a heartfelt showdown, he expresses his love for her and urges her to follow her heart, whether that leads her back to Brad or into the unknown with him. Touched by his sincerity, Jane musters the courage to admit her true feelings for Cooper, choosing a life filled with adventure and passion over the comfort of her previous path.

Epilogue with HEA - Jane and Cooper's POV

A year later, we find Jane settled on the ranch, fully embracing her new life as the co-owner alongside Cooper. As they work together, gathering and caring for the cattle, their bond grows stronger, bringing joy to the ranch and their hearts. Friends and family celebrate their love at a rustic barn wedding, surrounded by the beauty of the land they cherish. Jane reflects on how her journey led to a love that feels like home and a life she never thought possible. Together, they ride off into the sunset, ready to tackle whatever adventures life throws their way, hand-in-hand.

Title: Falling Hard for the Boss

Chapter 1: Intro to Heroine (Olivia Hart) - HER POV

Olivia Hart is introduced as a vibrant and creative project manager at Innovatech Solutions. Her carefree style, quick wit, and infectious enthusiasm make her a beloved figure within her team. However, beneath her outgoing approach is a fierce desire to prove herself in a male-dominated industry. The chapter captures her struggles and aspirations as she sets her sights on creating innovative solutions that challenge the status quo.

Chapter 2: Intro to Hero (Trent Caldwell) - HIS POV

Trent Caldwell is introduced as a rigorous and disciplined CEO, known for his corporate no-nonsense demeanor. He is dedicated to maintaining the company's high standards and productivity, believing that innovation must abide by strict guidelines. Through his perspective, readers learn of his backstory—a military background that ingrained him with a strong work ethic but left little room for personal relationships or emotional vulnerability.

Chapter 3: Meet Cute - HER POV

The two meet in a tense company meeting when Olivia pitches a bold idea for the upcoming project. Trent dismisses her ambitions outright, leading to a heated exchange that captures both their frustrations and competitive spirits. The chapter showcases their immediate chemistry, an initial attraction masked by their clashing personalities.

Chapter 4: Growing Attraction/Getting to Know Each Other - HIS POV

As the two are forced to collaborate on the project, they embark on a journey filled with misunderstandings, banter, and creative conflict. Olivia begins to see the human side of Trent—the passionate leader behind the tough exterior, while Trent learns about Olivia's unwavering determination and sparks of brilliance. Their late-night brainstorming sessions hint at a growing connection amid their initial friction.

Chapter 5: First Kiss - HER POV

After a late night of work, Olivia and Trent share a moment of vulnerability, revealing personal stories about their pasts. Overcome by emotions and the tension that has been building, they lean in and share their first kiss—a soft yet electrifying moment that ignites feelings they both were trying to suppress. The chapter alternates between their astonishment and excitement, capturing the thrill of what just happened.

Chapter 6: Her Smell - HIS POV

Trent becomes increasingly aware of Olivia's captivating presence, particularly her unique scent. As he works on their project, he finds himself distracted by her proximity and the aroma that lingers long after she leaves the room. His colleagues notice his infatuation, teasing him about the way he lights up whenever Olivia is around. This chapter highlights his growing crush and further complicates his previously strict demeanor.

Chapter 7: His Taste - HER POV

Meanwhile, Olivia reflects on the kiss while confiding in her best friend. She describes Trent's taste—how the kiss sent ripples of excitement through her body and left her with a sense of yearning. Her friend encourages her to embrace the burgeoning feelings, while Olivia grapples with her attraction, emphasizing her desire to maintain her independence.

Chapter 8: Internal Conflict/Resistance to Attraction - HIS POV

Both characters wrestle with their budding relationship. Olivia fears that getting close to Trent might compromise her career ambitions, while Trent struggles with the vulnerability that comes with opening up to someone. As their connection deepens, both throw up emotional barriers, worried about how their relationship might affect their professional roles. Tension rises as they navigate their growing feelings while keeping their guard up.

Chapter 9: Steamy Hot Intimate Scene - HER POV

After a night of celebrating their project's progress, the chemistry explodes as they find themselves alone. What starts as playful teasing turns into a steamy intimate scene that strips away their defenses, blending passion and desire. The chapter is filled with rich descriptions of their sensations, showcasing how they truly connect on an emotional and physical level—the moment redefines their relationship dynamics.

Chapter 10: Internal Falling in Love - HIS POV

As Olivia and Trent's relationship flourishes, they each have moments of realization about their feelings. Olivia discovers she can balance her individuality with love, while Trent allows himself to embrace emotions he resisted. Their playful banter, surprise moments, and small gestures illustrate their internal transformation and growing attachment.

Chapter 11: Dark Moment/Pulling Apart - HER POV

Just when they seemed to have struck a balance between love and work, a critical misunderstanding occurs. A major miscommunication leads to a rift when Trent chastises Olivia for a decision made on the project without consulting him. Hurt, Olivia feels sidelined and undervalued, leading her to question whether she should distance herself from him.

Chapter 12: Resolution - HIS POV

In the aftermath of their fight, Trent retreats into introspection, reflecting internally on his entrenchment in his corporate mindset and regrets.

Eventually, he and Olivia confront their misunderstandings and share heartfelt conversations, during which they communicate their emotions and fears. They realize their love is strong enough to overcome obstacles. They come together to resolve their issues, unearthing their vulnerabilities and deciding to support each other professionally and personally, clearing the path for a powerful partnership.

Epilogue with HEA - HER POV

A few months later, Trent and Olivia have launched the successful project, and their teamwork has fostered an innovative culture at Innovatech Solutions. Their bond has strengthened, and they navigate their romantic partnership with ease and joy. The epilogue features a light-hearted office celebration reflecting their accomplishments, culminating in Trent's public acknowledgment of Olivia as a vital partner, both in the office and in life, affirming their happily ever after together.

Title: Riding Into Tomorrow

Chapter 1: Lily's POV - Intro to Heroine

Lily Harper is introduced as a dedicated and compassionate physical therapist working at a rehabilitation center in Texas. She has a deep passion for helping people heal and recover, stemming from her own experiences with injury in her college athletics. Though dedicated to her career, she harbors an unfulfilled longing for a more adventurous life, often fantasizing about meeting someone who complements her heart.

Chapter 2: Marek's POV - Intro to Hero

Marek "Tempest" Wilson, a skilled and fearless bull rider, is introduced sharing memories from his glory days filled with adrenaline and excitement. His life revolves around the thrill of the rodeo and the camaraderie of fellow riders. While he appears confident and bold to the outside world, Marek internally struggles with the commitment and vulnerability required to experience deeper connections in his life.

Chapter 3: Meet Cute (Lily's POV)

Lily meets Marek for the first time when he arrives at the rehabilitation center post-accident with shattered legs. Their first interaction is marked by Marek's stubbornness—he tries to downplay his injuries, but Lily sees right through it. Despite the bitter circumstances, they share a moment of reluctant laughter that hints at the potential for a deeper connection.

Chapter 4: Growing Attraction/Getting to Know Each Other (Marek's POV)

As Marek goes through his physical therapy, he starts to admire Lily's dedication and perseverance. He notices the way her hair falls when she bends to help him, and her unwavering spirit sparks an attraction he's never known. Marek opens up about his life as a bull rider and his love for the rodeo, which captivates Lily's heart.

Chapter 5: First Kiss (Lily's POV)

During a particularly emotional therapy session, Marek shares his fears about not riding again, which strikes a chord in Lily. As they engage in a candid conversation, a moment of shared vulnerability ignites an undeniable chemistry between them. Leaning in, they share a brief but impactful kiss filled with feelings neither fully understands, throwing them both into confusion about their relationship.

Chapter 6: His Smell (Marek's POV)

While going through rehabilitation, Marek can't help but notice Lily's refreshing scent, a mix of lavender from her lotion and the slight musk that comes from the energy of working with athletes. The sensory reminder of her fills his thoughts and makes his heart race each time she steps close, prompting playful teasing from his fellow patients who observe the way he lights up around her.

Chapter 7: Her Taste (Lily's POV)

After their kiss, Lily finds herself replaying the moment in her mind. She confides in her best friend about the surge of emotions and the butterflies in her stomach. When her friend asks about Marek, Lily feels both excitement and trepidation over the kiss, as she contemplates whether pursuing Marek could risk their professional relationship.

Chapter 8: Internal Conflict/Resistance to Attraction (Marek's POV)

Marek battles with himself over his growing feelings for Lily. He worries about crossing boundaries and jeopardizing his healing process or her career. His internal struggle leads him to push her away emotionally, rationalizing that her support as a therapist is paramount and that he should focus solely on recovery rather than chasing feelings that could complicate everything.

Chapter 9: Steamy Hot Intimate Scene (Lily's POV)

In a heated moment after a breakthrough therapy session, Marek seeks solace in Lily's company, and she ends up waking feelings she can no longer ignore. They share an intimate connection that transcends the physical and emotional limitations they've faced. It's a passionate encounter filled with the promise of what could be, solidifying their bond.

Chapter 10: Internal Falling in Love (Marek's POV)

As Marek starts to regain his strength, he realizes his feelings for Lily have transformed from attraction into love. Memories of their deeper conversations, her support, and her unwavering dedication ignite a sense of hope within him. He yearns to share life with her outside the confines of therapy, imagining a future where they can navigate both the rodeo and life together.

Chapter 11: Dark Moment/Pulling Apart (Lily's POV)

Amidst their growing relationship, a sudden medical issue arises, bringing Marek's future and recovery into question. Fears about Marek's potential for a long-term future in bull riding resurface, and he pulls away emotionally, believing it's the only way to protect Lily from future heartache. Hurt and confusion plague Lily as she feels him slipping through her fingers.

Chapter 12: Resolution (Marek's POV)

After some soul-searching, Marek realizes he cannot bear to be without Lily and that love is worth the risk. He confronts his fears and reaches back out to her, expressing his feelings honestly. Together, they discuss not only their dreams and struggles but ways they can support each other. Their relationship emerges stronger through open communication, leading to a renewed commitment.

Epilogue: HEA (Lily's POV)

Months later, Marek is back in the arena, not only riding bulls but riding the waves of life with Lily by his side as his partner. They take on both challenges and triumphs together, cheering each other on while creating a loving home that fuses their worlds. The story concludes with

Marek riding his first bull again with Lily watching proudly from the background, embodying the love, passion, and resilience they've built together.

Outline for Rescue Mission

Chapter 1: Intro to Heroine (Juliet's POV)

Juliet Winters, a determined and free-spirited twenty-four-year-old, reflects on her life post-college graduation and her desire to break free from her father's protective grasp. While she appreciates his care, she can't stand the constant hovering from both her dad and his best friend, Nash. In her cozy studio apartment, she dreams of travel and adventure while sketching designs for her budding fashion line, contemplating whether her ambitions can coexist with the overbearing concern of the men in her life.

Chapter 2: Intro to Hero (Nash's POV)

Nash Reed, a charming and rugged architect in his late thirties, balances his successful career with the responsibility of being his best friend's confidant.Despite being ten years older than Juliet, he can't shake the feeling of wanting to protect her, especially after her recent family troubles. As he watches her navigate adulthood, he grapples with a growing awareness of his feelings for her, seeing her as more than just his friend's daughter but a woman worthy of love and respect.

Chapter 3: Meet Cute (Juliet's POV)

At her father's birthday party, Juliet runs into Nash in the backyard, where they both escape from the festivities for a breath of fresh air. Their playful banter leads to a lighthearted argument about her independence versus his desire to keep her safe. This moment reveals the undeniable spark between them, culminating in a shared laugh that lingers long after their playful squabble. The chemistry is undeniable but unacknowledged.

Chapter 4: Growing Attraction/Getting to Know Each Other (Nash's POV)

As Nash spends more time with Juliet amid her fashion line's preparations, their banter grows more flirtatious. Nash admires Juliet's creativity and passion, enjoying their shared moments of laughter and creativity. He learns that behind her bravado lies a heart looking for acceptance. His heart races as he feels an intense connection, forcing him to confront the reality of his feelings toward her.

Chapter 5: First Kiss (Juliet's POV)

One evening, while watching a fashion show on TV, Juliet and Nash engage in their usual witty repartee. Tension builds, and without thinking, she kisses him, shocked by the heat of the moment. The kiss ignites hidden emotions, leaving her breathless and questioning everything about their relationship. As they pull away, she sees confusion mingled with desire in Nash's eyes.

Chapter 6: Her Smell (Nash's POV)

The following day, as Nash works at his desk, the scent of lavender and citrus fills the air, triggering memories of Juliet after their kiss. The essence of her perfume wraps around him, reminding him of the warmth of her body close to his and her infectious laughter. One of his colleagues notices Nash's distraction and teases him about being smitten, leading him to brush it off but secretly embrace the truth.

Chapter 7: His Taste (Juliet's POV)

Later that week, Julie finds herself confiding in her best friend about the kiss. She recalls the thrilling surprise of the kiss—the way he tasted like warmth and confidence. Her heart races at the memory as she thinks about how Nash's lips felt against hers. Excited yet terrified, she contemplates what it means for their friendship and grapples with the possibility of taking a leap into the unknown.

Chapter 8: Internal Conflict/Resistance to Attraction (Nash's POV)

Despite his feelings deepening for Juliet, Nash battles his internal conflict. He feels guilty about wanting to pursue her, fearing he would betray his best friend or ruin their dynamic. This causes him to withdraw, offering encouragement without succumbing to the magnetic pull between them. He rationalizes his decision, telling himself that protecting her means creating emotional distance.

Chapter 9: Steamy Hot Intimate Scene (Juliet's POV)

During a late-night design session in her apartment, the tension between them surges as they get lost in conversation, sharing dreams and fears. Overwhelmed by emotion, they share another passionate kiss, this time more desperate and hungry. As clothing falls away, they explore each other in an intimate scene that awakens their deepest desires, intertwining their lives more than ever before.

Chapter 10: Internal Falling in Love (Nash's POV)

In the days following their steamy night, Nash begins to realize he is falling in love with Juliet. Every laugh, every glance, and every shared moment deepens his feelings. He recalls the way her passion shines when speaking about her clothing line and how she challenges him in ways he never expected. The warmth in his heart solidifies his realization: he can't walk away from her.

Chapter 11: Dark Moment/Pulling Apart (Juliet's POV)

When Juliet learns that Nash has pulled away again, fearing his emotional conflict, she feels a heartbreaking sense of loss. Believing she's lost the incredible connection they had, she withdraws, attempting to focus on her designs and forge her own path without him. Feeling abandoned, she confronts her father about his constant meddling, insisting she doesn't need rescuing. The argument heightens her sense of isolation.

Chapter 12: Resolution (Nash's POV)

Realizing the impact of his choices, Nash decides to confront both his feelings for Juliet and his fears head-on. He seeks her out, ready to fight for their connection and his love for her. In a heartfelt conversation, they air their grievances and insecurities, leading to a mutual understanding. Nash promises to support her independence while being present in her life in a new, more profound way.

Epilogue: HEA (Juliet's POV)

A year later, Juliet has successfully launched her fashion line, and Nash stands proudly at her opening gala. As the crowd cheers for her achievements, he steps away from the crowd to find her. They share an intimate moment, locked in each other's gaze, and Juliet feels the weight of his support and love. With a smile, she pulls him close, knowing they've built a bond so much stronger than either had anticipated. Together, they embrace their love, confident and free, ready for the adventure ahead.

Outline for Betting On Love

Chapter 1: Intro to Jamie (Heroine)

Jamie's POV: Introduce Jamie as a determined and ambitious young woman who is focused on her sports career. She's training for a big upcoming event and is often seen juggling workout schedules and her personal life. Show her interaction with friends, emphasizing her competitive nature and her no-nonsense attitude towards relationships, viewing love as a distraction.

Chapter 2: Intro to Tyler (Hero)

Tyler's POV: Introduce Tyler as the charming, easygoing friend who thrives on humor and light-heartedness. He's a natural athlete but prefers to enjoy the game rather than obsess over winning. Showcase his friendship with Jamie and provide insight into how their differing personalities have shaped their unlikely bond over the years.

Chapter 3: Meet Cute

Jamie's POV: At a local bar filled with sports enthusiasts, they both place a friendly wager on a game. Jamie dismisses Tyler's team, and Tyler challenges her audacity. Laughter ensues, and the playful rivalrous spirit of their friendship shines through. The bet is born, sparking the catalyst for the fake relationship.

Chapter 4: Growing Attraction/Getting to Know Each Other

Tyler's POV: As they begin the fake relationship, Tyler reflects on how amusing it is to see their friends' reactions. While attending a series of social events, the two grow closer. They share inside jokes, reminisce about past experiences, and engage in spontaneous adventures, leading Tyler to notice Jamie's hidden quirks and charm.

Chapter 5: First Kiss

Jamie's POV: After a night out where they fake a romantic engagement for their friends, Jamie feels an unexpected spark during a faux kiss. It catches her off guard, making her realize there's more to their arrangement. Jamie grapples with confusion over her feelings, questioning if there's truth behind the pretense.

Chapter 6: His Smell

Tyler's POV: As they watch a game at home, Tyler describes being acutely aware of Jamie's scent — her shampoo mixed with the freshness of her workout gear. The once unobtrusive smell now has him feeling inexplicably drawn to her, creating an intimate atmosphere that makes him reconsider what their relationship truly is.

Chapter 7: Her Taste

Jamie's POV:* As Jamie reflects on the kiss, she recalls how Tyler's lips tasted of warm vanilla and a hint of mint. It dawns on her that this sweetness contrasted sharply with her usual tough exterior. The kiss caught her completely off guard, igniting a fluttering feeling in her stomach that she had never anticipated. As she allows herself to replay that moment, Jamie realizes that tasting that sweetness kindled a dormant desire and ignited something deep inside her, making her question if she could allow herself to explore this new facet of their relationship. She grapples with a surprising longing to delve deeper into the intricacies of who Tyler really is, shifting her perspective from friend to something much more intimate.The kiss now feels like an invitation to a new level of intimacy she can't ignore.

Chapter 8: Internal Conflict/Resistance to Attraction

Tyler's POV: Despite his growing feelings, Tyler remains hesitant to accept he might want something deeper with Jamie. He battles speculation of ruining their friendship and worries about the possible fallout of a real relationship. Moments of insecurity trickle in, blurring his vision of what he thought was just a bet.

Chapter 9: Steamy Hot Intimate Scene

Jamie's POV: After a heated argument about their feelings over a recently attended event, tempers flare and passion ignites. They share a heated, intimate moment where boundaries are pushed, leading Jamie to embrace her feelings for Tyler, igniting desire that the two can no longer ignore.

Chapter 10: Internal Falling in Love

Tyler's POV: Tyler starts experiencing vivid realizations of love as he reflects on how Jamie's presence has changed his life. He thinks about how he considers their shared moments with a new depth, feeling as though pieces of his heart are attaching themselves to her, making him reluctant to pull away.

Chapter 11: Dark Moment/Pulling Apart

Jamie's POV: Just when they're learning to navigate their feelings, Jamie discovers that Tyler had initially planned for the bet to be just fun and games. Feeling hurt and betrayed, Jamie confronts him, leading to an emotional fallout. This revelation sends her into a spiral of doubt, causing her to pull away, fearing her heart is too vulnerable.

Chapter 12: Resolution

Tyler's POV: Tyler realizes that he cannot let their friendship slip away. He finds a way to apologize and show Jamie how much she means to him beyond the bet. After a heartfelt conversation filled with honesty and vulnerability, they address their feelings openly, leading them to a place of mutual understanding.

Epilogue: Happily Ever After (HEA)

Both POVs: Several months later, Tyler and Jamie are now happily together, navigating a real relationship with newfound depth and sincerity. They reminisce about how their playful bet transformed into a beautiful love story. Their friends celebrate their relationship as they prepare to attend an upcoming game, reflecting on the surprises life can bring when you least expect it.

Outline for Game Changers

Chapter 1: Intro to Heroine (Rachel Rosen)

Rachel's Perspective: Introduced as a savvy and ambitious sports agent, Rachel is driven by her past failures and the goal of carving out her place in the male-dominated industry. A master negotiator with a keen eye for talent, she is seen as both fierce and determined, ensuring that her athletes shine in the spotlight. However, she struggles with the pressure to maintain her reputation while yearning for true love.

Chapter 2: Intro to Hero (Brodan Thornton)

Brodan's Perspective: Brodan is the charismatic and well-connected sports agent with a golden touch. Known for his easygoing charm, he effortlessly navigates high-profile deals. Despite his success, he grapples with the superficiality of his lifestyle and fears that he's losing touch with what truly matters. Beneath his confident exterior lies an insecurities about sustaining his career amidst rising competition.

Chapter 3: Meet Cute

Rachel's Perspective: At a high-stakes football game where Alex Carter is playing, Rachel and Brodan inadvertently bump into each other while headed for the same scout meeting. Their initial sparks of rivalry flare as they exchange sharp words over who gets the first chance to approach Alex. This encounter sets the tone for their competitive relationship.

Chapter 4: Growing Attraction/Getting to Know Each Other

Brodan's Perspective: After their rocky start, Brodan finds himself oddly intrigued by Rachel's tenacity and brilliance. As he observes her chasing Alex, he begins to appreciate the layers of her character—her passion, her wit, and her determination. During a joint event they both attend, Brodan notices her in a new light, and their banter becomes electrifying.

Chapter 5: First Kiss

Rachel's Perspective: Forced to attend a charity gala together to present Alex as a candidate, Rachel and Brodan share a moment of vulnerability after a chaotic evening. An unexpected moment beneath the stars leads to their first kiss, igniting an undeniable chemistry. Though they both pull back, knowing their rivalry complicates things, they can't ignore the connection formed during that brief encounter.

Chapter 6: Her Smell

Brodan's Perspective: As they collaborate to keep Alex from spiraling during media scrutiny, Brodan can't help but be captivated by Rachel's scent—an alluring mix of fresh citrus and a hint of jasmine. It's a scent that clings to him during their late-night meetings, stirring up feelings he fails to acknowledge amid the chaos of their careers.

Chapter 7: His Taste

Rachel's Perspective: Late one night while strategizing over takeout and caffeine, Rachel tastes the sheer determination behind Brodan's convincing pitch for Alex's future. It's the combination of flavor and their shared ideas that magnifies her attraction rather than dulling it. With every laugh and engaging conversation, she feels walls beginning to crumble, both in her career and heart.

Chapter 8: Internal Conflict/Resistance to Attraction

Brodan's Perspective: As they grow closer, Brodan faces a dilemma of his own—can he balance his budding feelings for Rachel with the fierce competition that exists between them? Torn between wanting to take their relationship further and fearing it would undermine his career, he withdraws, leading to tension-filled meetings and unspoken tensions.

Chapter 9: Steamy Hot Intimate Scene

Rachel's Perspective: During a particularly stressful week managing Alex's negotiations, Rachel calls Brodan to vent frustration. What begins as a phone call quickly escalates into a heated moment as he arrives at her apartment. Their suppressed feelings culminate in a passionate encounter, leaving both breathless and even more conflicted about where they stand.

Chapter 10: Internal Falling in Love

Brodan's Perspective: The more they collaborate, the more Brodan realizes just how deeply he cares for Rachel. He admires her fierce loyalty to her clients and her dedication to doing right by Alex. As they share confidences and dreams, it dawns on him that this rivalry has subtly morphed into something more profound—something that looks suspiciously like love.

Chapter 11: Dark Moment/Pulling Apart

Rachel's Perspective: Just as things seem to be coming to a head, a scandal breaks involving Alex's personal life. In the chaos, Rachel discovers that Brodan received a tip-off about the issue from a rival agency and didn't inform her. Feeling betrayed, Rachel retreats from their partnership, convinced that their rivalry has hurt everyone involved.

Chapter 12: Resolution

Brodan's Perspective: Realizing the ramifications of their broken communication, Brodan reaches out to Rachel to explain his intentions. He admits his own mistakes and reveals that his feelings for her were genuine, not just a play for victory. Together, they devise a unified response to salvage Alex's future without compromising their integrity, working together and reclaiming their sparked emotions.

Epilogue: Happy Ever After (HEA)

Rachel and Brodan's Perspectives: Several months later, Alex's career is flourishing, and Rachel and Brodan's partnership has transitioned into a relationship. They stand side by side in a new venture of their own, officially partners in both business and life. Reflecting on their journey, they realize that sometimes love can bloom from the fiercest of rivalries, leading to a passion greater than any they had anticipated. They look forward to a future filled with challenges and triumphs, together.

Title: Not Too Shy for Love

Chapter 1: Intro to Heroine - Emily's POV

Emily Wilson is introduced on her first day of college, surrounded by a sea of unfamiliar faces. She reflects on her shyness and previously introverted nature, contemplating her decision to step out of her comfort zone. Emily's love for books and her dreams of finding acceptance and success in a new environment are established, alongside her determination to seize this opportunity for change.

Chapter 2: Intro to Hero - Alex's POV

Alex Thompson is introduced as the college's star quarterback, revered by his peers for both his athletic talent and his larger-than-life persona. However, beneath the confident facade lies a more vulnerable side; he feels pressured to maintain his image and struggles with understanding what he truly wants outside of football. Alex's background and desire for genuine connection are interwoven with his popularity and the expectations placed upon him.

Chapter 3: Meet Cute - Emily's POV

Emily accidentally bumps into Alex while rushing to class, causing her to drop her books. As they pick up the mess, they share a brief yet impactful moment filled with awkwardness and chemistry. Alex's charm and playful banter catch Emily off guard, leaving her flustered and intrigued, a stark contrast to her usual reserve. This serendipitous meeting sets the tone for their budding connection.

Chapter 4: Growing Attraction/Getting to Know Each Other - Alex's POV

As the semester progresses, Alex starts noticing Emily more around campus and finds himself drawn to her unique personality and intellect. After catching her in the library, he strikes up conversations with her, sharing laughs and moments that allow them to connect on a deeper level. Alex admires her resilience and authenticity, igniting a growing attraction as their interactions become more frequent.

Chapter 5: First Kiss - Emily's POV

During a late study session at the campus coffee shop, the atmosphere becomes charged as Emily and Alex delve into personal topics—dreams, fears, and hopes. As they lean closer, drawn by an invisible force, their surroundings fade away until their lips finally meet in a breathtaking first kiss filled with vulnerability and emotion. It's a pivotal moment for both, marking the start of something more significant.

Chapter 6: Her Smell - Alex's POV

Alex can't shake the memory of Emily after their kiss. He finds himself captivated by her presence, particularly the floral scent of her shampoo that lingers in his mind. In a humorous moment with his teammates, they notice his distracted demeanor and tease him about falling hard for the quiet girl whom he can't seem to stop thinking about. Despite the jokes, Alex realizes just how deeply she's embedded herself in his heart.

Chapter 7: His Taste - Emily's POV

After their first kiss, Emily confides in her best friend about her feelings for Alex. She recalls the taste of his lips, the warmth of the kiss igniting a whirlwind of emotions within her. Despite feeling exhilarated, she grapples with uncertainty about her attractiveness as her true self. Is she the person Alex is genuinely interested in, or just a facade she created? This self-doubt sets the stage for deeper inner conflict.

Chapter 8: Internal Conflict/Resistance to Attraction - Alex's POV

Though Alex is enchanted by Emily, he struggles with the contrast between his life as a popular athlete and the quieter, more introspective world Emily represents. He fears exposing her to the chaotic demands of his life, unsure if he can balance his responsibilities with a genuine relationship. This internal battle leads him to pull back slightly, leaving Emily confused and concerned.

Chapter 9: Steamy Hot Intimate Scene - Emily's POV

During an impromptu movie night at Alex's dorm, their playful banter soon ignites a chemistry that escalates into passionate heat. In the intimate comfort of the space and with the flickering light from the television, they share an undeniable connection, leading to a moment of deeper intimacy as they explore the boundaries of their relationship. Emily feels liberated yet nervous about how this will change their dynamic.

Chapter 10: Internal Falling in Love - Alex's POV

As their romance deepens, Alex begins to recognize that he's falling head over heels in love with Emily. He admires her quirks, her laughter, and her steadfastness despite her insecurities. During a quiet moment together, he realizes that their connection transcends social status, and he begins to envision a future with her—one where he feels authentic and accepted for who he truly is.

Chapter 11: Dark Moment/Pulling Apart - Emily's POV

Just when things feel perfect, a misunderstanding arises when Emily overhears Alex discussing his perfect girlfriend with friends, assuming he means someone else. Hurt and feeling like she's not worthy of his love, Emily withdraws from Alex, leading to a painful distance between them. She grapples with her sense of identity, questioning whether she made the right choice in changing herself to fit into Alex's world.

Chapter 12: Resolution - Alex's POV

Alex, feeling the void left by Emily's absence, gathers the courage to confront her. He clarifies his feelings, emphasizing that it is her true self he is drawn to, not an idealized version. In an emotional reunion, he professes his love, assuring her that he values her for who she is. Together, they embrace authenticity, vowing to support each other's dreams and personalities moving forward.

Epilogue with HEA - Emily and Alex's POV

A few months later, Emily and Alex are shown thriving together in their relationship, enjoying the richness of their unique bond. They celebrate their first anniversary at a quaint café where they first shared their hopes and dreams. Surrounded by friends and laughter, they reflect on how they've both grown, grateful for the love they've found—one that accepts and cherishes their true selves. Hand in hand, they look forward to their future, confident in their commitment to being authentic together.

Outline for Behind the Bear

Chapter 1: Intro to Heroine - Jess's POV

Jessica Harper is introduced as the school's spirited mascot, a role she takes pride in despite the heat of the heavy bear costume. As she navigates high school life, she feels invisible—often overlooked by her classmates, especially the popular crowd. Despite her vibrant personality, Jess struggles with self-esteem and craves recognition beyond her fuzzy façade. She reflects on her dreams of being known for something more substantial, expressing her fears of being trapped in a costume rather than showing her true self.

Chapter 2: Intro to Hero - Lucas's POV

Lucas Reed, the star basketball player, is introduced on the court, exuding confidence and charm. He is used to attention for his skills on the court and feels the pressure to maintain his cool, popular image. Behind the confident exterior, he feels the weight of expectations from his team and family. Lucas's inner thoughts reveal his desire for genuine connections but fear losing his reputation. He's not just a jock; he yearns for deeper relationships and understanding.

Chapter 3: Meet Cute - Jess's POV

During a halftime break, Jess has a moment of vulnerability as she battles the heat while removing her bear head in the locker room. Unbeknownst to her, Lucas walks in, and upon seeing her in casual clothes, he is taken aback. Jess realizes she has been caught unguarded, unsure how to react. Their eyes meet, and Jess instinctively feels a rush of embarrassment while Lucas, genuinely surprised, offers a compliment that leaves her flustered and intrigued.

Chapter 4: Growing Attraction/Getting to Know Each Other - Lucas's POV

After their unexpected encounter, Lucas can't shake the image of Jess from his mind. Intrigued by her spirit, he starts looking for opportunities to talk, offering encouragement in passing and joining her during mascot practice. It becomes a playful back-and-forth, and Lucas starts to admire her determination. As their chemistry grows, he realizes he may be falling for the girl behind the bear.

Chapter 5: First Kiss - Jess's POV

When Jess invites Lucas to help her with mascot routines one evening, their playful banter culminates in an unexpected first kiss. In that electric moment, Jess feels a whirlwind of emotions—confidence mingled with surprise and delight. The kiss awakens feelings she never fully acknowledged, and she spends the night replaying the moment, her heart racing. Jess confides in her best friend about the kiss, expressing confusion about her newfound feelings.

Chapter 6: Her Smell - Lucas's POV

As weeks pass, Lucas finds himself enchanted by Jess, particularly how she smells—an intoxicating mix of her shampoo and the faint scent of fresh cotton from her clothes. He realizes how deeply he desires to be close to her while studying for an upcoming game. During practice, a teammate playfully nudges him, teasingly asking if he's lovestruck, prompting Lucas to realize how strong his feelings have become. The teasing makes him both bashful and excited.

Chapter 7: His Taste - Jess's POV

After sharing that unforgettable kiss, Jess can't help but replay it in her mind. She describes the taste of Lucas's lips and how they made her feel to her best friend during their late-night gossip sessions. Jess is still grappling with her self-image and worries that Lucas might lose interest when he sees her true self. Conflicted but excited, Jess cherishes the warmth of the kiss as an escape from her insecurities.

Chapter 8: Internal Conflict/Resistance to Attraction - Lucas's POV

Lucas struggles with his feelings for Jess, torn between pursuing her and adhering to the social expectations of being a popular athlete. He worries that dating someone like Jess could change how others perceive him. One day, his friends mention having a party, subtly pushing him towards other girls. His heart is pulling him towards Jess, but the pressures from his social circle leave him feeling conflicted and hesitant.

Chapter 9: Steamy Hot Intimate Scene - Jess's POV

When Jess and Lucas find themselves alone during a school dance, the electric tension snaps as they break through their barriers, engaging in a heated, passionate moment that is both exhilarating and liberating. The intimacy of the dance leads to a deeper connection, where Jess feels cherished and beautiful. She immerses herself in the experience, realizing her insecurities melt away when she's in Lucas's presence. This moment shapes her understanding of love and desire.

Chapter 10: Internal Falling in Love - Lucas's POV

Lucas finds himself Daydreaming about Jess; he recognizes that his feelings have grown much deeper than infatuation. He admires her spirit, humor, and kindness—qualities that make him feel grounded. Reflecting on an upcoming game, he can't imagine celebrating without Jess by his side. Lucas begins to crave a genuine relationship, hoping to create a bond that transcends high school stereotypes.

Chapter 11: Dark Moment/Pulling Apart - Jess's POV

When rumors spread about Lucas dating a popular cheerleader, Jess's insecurities resurface. Feeling betrayed and uncertain of where she stands, she confronts Lucas about the rumors. Lucas's inability to succinctly dismiss the gossip only adds to her heartache, leading Jess to withdraw emotionally. Conflicted, Jess decides to put distance between them, believing it's best not to get hurt again.

Chapter 12: Resolution - Lucas's POV

Realizing he doesn't want to lose Jess, Lucas confronts her directly, laying bare his feelings. He admits he's been pushed by friends but has only ever wanted to be with her. Through a heartfelt exchange, they discuss their fears, insecurities, and what they truly want. This openness reignites their connection, leading to a moment of reconciliation where they choose each other, affirming their love.

Epilogue with HEA - Jess's POV

Several months later, Jess and Lucas are happily navigating a relationship that embraces both their differences and shared passions. With Jess gaining confidence as the mascot and Lucas thriving on the basketball court, they attend games together, celebrating accomplishments side by side. Jess reflects on the journey that brought them together, filled with laughter, love, and a deep understanding of each other, solidifying their bond beyond high school. They celebrate their first anniversary, marking the beginning of many more adventures together, fully embracing who they are—together.

50 Names for Romance Heroines

Brainstorm names that make your romance heroines come alive. Here are a few starters!

1. Amelia
2. Sophia
3. Ella
4. Zoe
5. Lila
6. Clare
7. Mila
8. Aria
9. Charlotte "Charlie"
10. Isla
11. Ruby
12. Keanna
13. Maya
14. Sienna
15. Tessa
16. Emily
17. Evie
18. Hannah
19. Cleopatra "Cleo"
20. Savannah Rose
21. Dahlia
22. Keira
23. Jasmine
24. Fiona

25. Sienna
26. Bethany
27. Hayley
28. Amara
29. Leanne
30. Rylie
31. Whitney
26. Violet
27. Megan
28. Lydia
29. Autumn
30. Sophie
31. Gwen
32. Poppy
33. Ivy
34. Cecilia
35. Selena
36. Rory
38. Gabriella "Gabby"
39. Alyssa
40. Madeline "Maddie"
41. Elena
42. Kaya
43. Brooke
44. Danielle "Dani"
45. Talia
46. Phoebe
47. Luna
48. Chloe
49. Sierra
50. Leigh

These names evoke charm and strength, making them perfect for captivating heroines in romance novels!

50 Names for Romance Heroes

Brainstorm names that make your romance heroes stand out. Here are a few starters!

1. Liam
2. Ethan
3. Jack
4. Maxwell "Max"
5. Asher
6. Brixton "Brix"
7. Caleb
8. Ronan
9. Wyatt
10. Logan
11. Oliver
12. Jasper
13. Nico
14. Dylan
15. Finn
16. Luke
17. Aiden
18. Carter
19. Silas
20. Gabriel "Gabe"
21. Sebastian
22. Grayson "Gray"
23. Zachary "Zach"
24. Flynt

25. Blake
26. Hunter
27. Luca
28. Julian
29. Ryder
30. Tristan
31. Dante
32. Kellan
33. Jaxon "Jax"
34. Milo
35. Theo
36. Samir
38. Weston "Wes"
39. Dominic "Dom"
40. Kieran
41. Spencer
42. Chase
43. Gideon
44. Parker
45. Sullivan "Sully"
46. Nash
47. Rex
48. Jett
49. Damon
50. Reid

These names can add depth and charisma to your romance heroes, providing a variety of personalities and backgrounds for your stories!

Extra Bonus 1
25 Ways for Couples to Meet In a Romance

Brainstorm creative ways for your couple to meet. Here are a few starters!

1. Bookstore Encounter: They reach for the same rare book on a dusty shelf and spark a conversation about their favorite authors.

2. Dating App Mix Up: She/He mistakes her/him for her/his online date.

3. The Cute Lift: He sees her struggling with a hefty piece of furniture or a hefty delivery into her apartment, and like a gentleman he offers to help.

4. Cooking Class: Both sign up for a gourmet cooking class and find themselves paired together, leading to flour fights and culinary chemistry.

5. Second-Hand Store: They bump into each other while searching for vintage clothes and end up modeling outfits for each other in front of a mirror.

6. New Year's Smooch: They're the only non-couple at a New Year's Eve party, and for good luck they agree to kiss each other when the clock strikes midnight.

7. Dog Park: Their dogs become fast friends, leading to a series of awkward but cute encounters as they both try to rein in their excited pets.

8. Rideshare: They share a ride from the airport.

9. Travel Mix-Up: They accidentally switch bags at an airport and realize they're headed to the same retreat, leading to unexpected adventures together.

10. Local Farmers Market: They strike up a conversation while sampling produce, discovering shared tastes that lead to an impromptu picnic.

11. Community Garden: They're neighbors in a community garden, sparking a rivalry over whose vegetables grow better that leads to shared gardening tips and flirting.

12. Trivia Night: Both are contestants at a local trivia night, leading to witty banter and eventual team-up as they try to win together.

13. Ghostwriting Job: They're both hired to ghostwrite the same celebrity's biography, leading to playful one-upmanship and accidental coffee spills.

14. Music Festival: They meet at a music festival, bonding over the same artist they both adore and sharing a dance under the stars.

15. Family Wedding: They meet as plus-ones at a chaotic family wedding, forced to navigate family antics together.

16. Art Exhibition: They strike up a conversation while admiring the same controversial piece of art, leading to a spirited debate and deeper connection.

17. Ski Resort: They're both beginners at a ski resort, continually falling and helping each other up, creating a bond filled with laughter.

18. Themed Costume Party: They both come dressed as rival characters from the same movie and engage in playful banter that leads to unexpected chemistry.

19. Grocery Store Mishap: They accidentally cart-crash in a grocery store, leading to a humorous debate on who gets the last box of their favorite cereal.

20. Hot Air Balloon Ride: They are both on a hot air balloon ride that becomes unexpectedly scary, bonding over their shared thrill and fear as they float above the world.

21. Charity Auction: They are both bidding on the same item at a charity auction and end up competing in a humorous and flirtatious way.

22. Yoga Class: They mistakenly end up in the wrong yoga class and bond over their shared lack of flexibility and awkward poses.

23. Fantasy Convention: Both are fans of the same fantasy series, leading to an intense discussion about plot twists that turns into a fun adventure in convention activities.

24. Art Gallery Opening: They each attend an art gallery opening looking for inspiration, but instead, they find inspiration in each other's opinions on the exhibits.

25. Fishing Trip: They're paired as fishing buddies on a group trip, facing the challenges of nature while slowly peeling back each other's layers.

Extra Bonus 2

25 Settings for Scenes In Short Romances

Brainstorm unique scenes for your short romance. Here are a few starters!

Here are 25 unique settings that can serve as captivating backdrops for scenes in a romance novel:

1. Vintage Train: A scenic journey through the countryside on a beautifully restored train, with shared compartments sparking intimate conversations.

2. Botanical Garden: Amidst vibrant flowers and serene ponds, a couple navigates a maze of flora, finding beauty and romance in every corner.

3. Hidden Beach Cove: A secluded beach only accessible by a rocky path, where two characters discover tranquility and unguarded moments together.

4. Snow-Covered Cabin: Cozy nights by the fire in a rustic cabin, surrounded by winter's serenity, provide the perfect opportunity for heart-to-heart talks.

5. Art Studio: In a sun-drenched art studio, surrounded by splashes of color and creativity, their shared passion for art unveils hidden emotions.

6. Amusement Park: The thrill of rides, lingering smiles over cotton candy, and the magic of nighttime fireworks create an atmosphere of joy and excitement.

7. Lighthouse: Perched on a cliff, an old lighthouse serves as a picturesque setting for soul-stirring conversations against the crashing ocean waves.

8. Rooftop Garden: A city rooftop adorned with lush plants and twinkling lights offers a private escape for two amidst the bustling urban landscape.

9. Historical Manor: A grand manor steeped in history, where secrets linger in the air, leading to romantic escapades and mysterious discoveries.

10. Jazz Club: The sultry atmosphere of a jazz club, with live music and dim lighting, provides the perfect backdrop for soulful dancing and flirtation.

11. Street Festival: The lively energy of a local street festival, filled with music, dancing, and street food, ignites the passion in spontaneous encounters.

13. Winery: In a picturesque vineyard, they savor wine tastings and learn about each other's lives while exploring the enchanting surroundings.

14. Ice Skating Rink: A charming outdoor ice skating rink adorned with twinkling lights creates an enchanting atmosphere for playful falls and intimate moments.

15. Lavender Field: A stunning lavender field in full bloom enchants them as they stroll through the fragrant rows, evoking romance and delightful daydreams.

16. Countryside Picnic: A spontaneous picnic in a flower-filled meadow, where a blanket, homemade sandwiches, and the vast sky create a laid-back atmosphere for connection.

17. Floating Market: A vibrant floating market filled with colorful boats and delicious street food sets the stage for unexpected encounters and cultural exchanges.

18. Surfboard Rental Shop: A laid-back coastal rental shop where they bond over shared laughter and surfing challenges, catching waves and feelings.

19. An Abandoned Amusement Park: The beauty of nostalgia and decaying rides forms an eerie yet romantic backdrop, igniting their adventurous spirits.

20. Meditation Retreat: A tranquil setting in the mountains for inner reflection and renewed connection, where mindfulness opens pathways to each other's hearts.

21. Sailing Yacht: A romantic getaway on a yacht where they're surrounded by the sea, discovering a synergy amidst the waves.

22. Escape Room: Locked in a themed escape room, their synergy and teamwork create an unexpected spark, as they unravel puzzles and each other's hearts.

23. Mountain Hiking Trail: Amidst breathtaking views and the invigorating scent of pine, a challenging hike leads to moments of vulnerability and growing attraction.

24. Medieval Fair: At a lively medieval fair, complete with jousting, craft stalls, and festive food, characters engage in playful competitions and romantic mischief.

25. Haunted House Tour: In a thrilling haunted house, their shared fright results in laughter and closeness as they navigate twists, turns, and surprises together.

~ **Thanks for Reading!** ~

I hope you enjoyed the book
And the extra bonuses.
Best to You
On All Your Writing
Endeavors – Paige

www.ingramcontent.com/pod-product-compliance
Lightning Source LLC
Chambersburg PA
CBHW050508160726

48003CB00001B/218